FREEDOM FROM EMOTIONAL EATING

For more information on Paul McKenna and his books,
see his website at www.paulmckenna.com

www.**transworldbooks**.co.uk

FREEDOM FROM EMOTIONAL EATING

•

PAUL McKENNA PH.D.

EDITED BY HUGH WILLBOURN PH.D.

BANTAM PRESS

LONDON · TORONTO · SYDNEY · AUCKLAND · JOHANNESBURG

TRANSWORLD PUBLISHERS
61–63 Uxbridge Road, London W5 5SA
A Random House Group Company
www.transworldbooks.co.uk

First published in Great Britain
in 2014 by Bantam Press
an imprint of Transworld Publishers

A CIP catalogue record for this book
is available from the British Library.

ISBN 9780593064078

Addresses for Random House Group Ltd companies outside the UK
can be found at: www.randomhouse.co.uk
The Random House Group Ltd Reg. No. 954009

The Random House Group Limited supports the Forest Stewardship Council® (FSC®), the
leading international forest-certification organisation. Our books carrying the FSC label are
printed on FSC®-certified paper. FSC is the only forest-certification scheme supported by
the leading environmental organisations, including Greenpeace. Our paper procurement
policy can be found at www.randomhouse.co.uk/environment

Designed and typeset by Julia Lloyd
Printed and bound in Great Britain by
Clays Ltd, Bungay, Suffolk

2 4 6 8 10 9 7 5 3 1

MIX
Paper from
responsible sources
FSC® C016897

CONTENTS

READ THIS FIRST

You hold in your hands an extraordinary book that in just a few days can change your life for ever! This is more than just a book, it is a system that has taken me years to develop, and which I have tested over and over again, with consistent and astounding results. So please make sure you use every part of it.

There are just six elements you have to use:

In the book:

1. **Read the book from cover to cover, follow the instructions and use the Success Tracker at the back.**

On the DVD:

2. **Watch the DVD and do the Havening Technique with me every day for the next five days. It is just like a personal session with me, which will give you the power to take charge of your emotions.**

On the CD:

3. **Listen to the Hypnotic Trance every day for the next seven days, and thereafter whenever you feel you need it. I will put hypnotic suggestions deep into your subconscious mind that make you automatically get more control over your emotions and your food.**

4. **Put on the 'Listen While You Eat' track while you are eating for the next seven days, to train your brain automatically to feel more in control around food, so that you eat less without feeling like you are missing out.**

5. **Use the Stopping Self-Sabotage technique: it's amazingly simple and will change any subconscious beliefs that are stopping you from succeeding.**

6. **Finally, use the Emotional Balancing technique, a breakthrough technique that will give you the emotional freedom that liberates you from food.**

All these elements combine to make my system, which the research studies show is the most effective weight-loss system in the world.

We will spend a few quality minutes a day together for the next seven days. Together we are going to change your thinking and behaviour at the most fundamental level so that you lose weight, you feel in control around your emotions, you access your deepest sense of wisdom, and you are free to experience joy, happiness and emotional prosperity.

Overview

The book is laid out so that as you read through it, you integrate the steps you need, and they build on each other one at a time.

- **Chapters One, Two and Three, the Trance and the DVD, give you all the tools you need to set out on this adventure of transformation. The process really is life-changing. The techniques in the Trance and the Havening video will help you achieve these changes and keep you safe and secure as they occur.**

- **Chapters Four and Five are the zone of change. You are going to recalibrate your emotional responses and you will come out the far side changed for the better. You will remove habitual patterns that have been holding you back from achieving your full potential and your healthy natural weight. You will finally be free to live up to your full potential.**

- **Chapters Six and Seven are your guide to life with the full wealth, challenge and reward of your emotional experience and wisdom. Tuning in to the emotional channels that were blocked off by emotional eating is like adding another dimension to your life. It can be as dramatic as changing a film**

from 2D to 3D or taking a picture in black and white and adding colour.

This whole system will cause a physiological change in your brain chemistry that affects you far more than mere weight loss. You will get a massive sense of relief. You will be able to show up for life alert, flexible, relaxed and optimistic because the landscape of your brain has been reset to a higher and happier level of functioning.

Turn the page and start the journey!

FREEDOM FROM EMOTIONAL EATING

CHAPTER ONE

•

An Amazing Breakthrough

An amazing breakthrough

Would you like to join me on an extraordinary journey? Do you feel that you have tried just about every way there is to lose weight, but the success never lasts? Are you ever frustrated? Do you find yourself eating when you are not hungry? Are you ready to try something new? If so, I honestly believe I can help you.

You will be able to eat whatever you want, yet not to excess. You will be healthy and revitalized at a vibrant, slim weight. Emotions that were confusing, overwhelming or repetitive will be transformed and leave you with joy, optimism and understanding.

Wherever you are – at home, in a bookshop, on a train or on a beach – I'm inviting you to join me right now on an extraordinary, exciting, life-changing journey. You don't have to climb a mountain, trek through a jungle or sail around the world, yet at the end of this journey you will have totally new behaviours around food.

Even more amazing, not only you, but all the world around you will have changed. Problems you thought were fixed and unchangeable will have disappeared. Goals that seemed unattainable will soon be counted among your achievements. You will find that the whole world really is rich and full of possibilities.

This may sound exciting or a bit scary, or unbelievable, and it is more than likely that at some point this journey will appear to be all of these, but every step of the way I will be with you in this book, CD and DVD to be your guide and companion as you lose weight and gain emotional control.

Whatever your situation, now that you have started reading, you are in exactly the right place to begin this magnificent process of change. You are going to achieve a level of healthiness and awareness you cannot yet imagine. Welcome to a great adventure!

Why I had to write this book

I have been helping people to lose weight for over fifteen years and I honestly thought I had no more to learn about weight loss. However, in the last two years there has been an extraordinary scientific breakthrough in controlling emotional overwhelm. I am fortunate to have been working closely with Dr Ronald Ruden at the cutting edge of this new technology.

The approach we are using has been hailed as a significant advance in the understanding and treatment of the neurochemistry of emotions. I believe we have cracked the code for emotional equilibrium and sustainable weight loss.

Emotional eating is the number-one cause of excessive weight gain. We now have a procedure that reduces overwhelming emotions, resets your brain chemistry and restores emotional health. Being overweight is not an accident. Success and happiness are not accidents. Everything has a cause, and we have tracked down the most common underlying cause of excess weight, and how to lose it comfortably and permanently.

Dr Ruden and I have used his technique on more than a thousand people, and it works over and over again without any side effects. We've worked with relationship issues, post-traumatic stress disorder, depression and many other conditions. The work with emotional eaters in particular has been almost miraculous. They have all been able to move away from stress, anxiety and excess weight, and towards feeling calm and in control with healthy, sustained weight loss.

How this book is different

I've already written two books that successfully help people lose weight. *I Can Make You Thin*, first published in 2005, is the best-selling weight-loss book in British history, and has now sold over three million copies worldwide.

Hypnotic Gastric Band, published in 2012, has already helped hundreds of thousands of people who believed nothing could help them achieve a slim, healthy body. The hypnotic gastric band convinces the mind to make the body automatically eat less.

So I can understand why people might say, 'Paul, do you really need to write another book about weight loss?'

If we were focusing just on that, I would have to answer, 'No.'

If all you want is to lose weight, then *I Can Make You Thin* has everything you need, and if you require an extra boost or a helping hand, then using *Hypnotic Gastric Band* will help you lose weight swiftly and safely.

But I see this book as the missing bit of the jigsaw. Here we address the emotions underlying excess eating. Of all the things I help people with, weight loss is my favourite. I don't have all the answers, but I do have an immense enthusiasm for this new breakthrough, and I want to share it so that as many people as possible can lose weight safely, permanently and enjoyably. Because when you are free from emotional eating, you are not just slimmer, you are happier!

This system releases the emotional wisdom and sensitivity that has been suppressed beneath the habit of emotional eating. You will feel better and you will move to a healthy, thin body weight because now we are getting to the root cause of the problem, with a healing process that frees you from patterns that started deep in your past. When you overcome emotional eating, losing weight is only one element of a far bigger change.

Of course, a cynic could still say, 'Surely if people lose weight that will make them feel better anyway. You don't need another book.'

And I can reply, 'Well, for some people, you are right. Because the fact is that millions of people *do* lose weight using my system, and they *do* feel better and *they* don't need this book. They are happy at their new weight, they are happy in themselves and they are getting on with their lives just fine. They have ups and downs just like all the rest of us and they carry on fine.'

This system is created specifically for you, if you are an emotional eater. You don't just want to lose weight, you want something more. You want a better relationship with your own emotions and you want to eliminate once and for all the cause of your overeating. This system is not just remedial. It is for people who want a richer life and freedom of choice: freedom to eat what they really desire, and to feel the full benefit of their emotional wisdom.

Why does this system work so well?

This system is successful because it works with the natural intelligence of your body. It restores the body's natural method to keep itself fit and healthy, and shows you how to comfortably process all of your emotions.

I firmly believe that if you are overweight, it is not your fault. It's not. It is the fault of your programming.

All your decisions about what you eat, when you eat and how much you eat are made in your brain. Your brain is like a computer: it can be programmed. In the past, your brain was running you. As you use this system, together we are going to reprogram the way you think and act around food.

Using the power of hypnosis and calming psychosensory techniques, we go directly to your unconscious mind to rewrite those programs. Inside one week, this system can totally reprogram your behaviour around food. Many people say it is like a switch has been flipped in their brain and they simply don't have compulsions around eating any more.

You will also be given a simple and powerful way to work with your emotions. Feelings that were strange or frightening or just too painful will become completely manageable and even rewarding. So-called 'negative' emotions will be transformed into a pathway to greater insight and security. You will no longer feel out of control. Your emotional world will become a source of strength which helps you move towards real satisfaction in all areas of your life.

Diets are the problem

Most importantly, this system works because it is not a diet. This system is a process of psychological and behavioural change. When I suggested fifteen years ago that diets were rubbish and the key to weight loss was in the mind, I felt like a lone voice in the wilderness. Now there is an army of doctors who believe that diets are the problem. Research has shown that for 84 per cent of people, diets don't work. Just recently, another study by researchers from Yale, the leading university in America, concluded that obesity should be treated as a behavioural problem.

Diets are worse than useless, they are actually creating the problem. Over time, they cause people to gain weight. Millions of people have tried diets and the research shows that the vast majority end up gaining weight.

Diet clubs and food substitutes have been relentlessly advertised and grown into a massive market over the last forty years. During that time, obesity has grown from a fringe problem to the biggest threat to health and the biggest healthcare cost in the Western world.

No one puts on five stone overnight. They have usually gone from one diet to another. At first they lose weight and think they are being successful, but in reality they are starving themselves, and they pay the price of slowing their metabolism by gaining yet more weight when they stop the diet.

Every person I have met with a serious weight problem

has dieted their way to obesity. Diets push the body into survival mode. They require people to consciously restrain their food intake to a starvation diet. As soon as the dieter relaxes for an instant, the body tries to recover from starvation by eating to lay down fat to protect itself. As a result, 70 per cent of dieters end up heavier than when they started. When people try one diet after another, sooner or later they end up in that 70 per cent. I believe diets and diet clubs are a rip-off at every level. As far as I'm concerned, they don't work, they make the problem worse and they take your money.

For fifteen years I have advocated a different approach, and two independent studies have verified it works for seven out of ten people who use it. With this new approach to emotional eating, I believe we can make that proportion even higher. I look forward to you being the next success story.

This system isn't like a diet, which stops working and causes you to binge. This system can't stop working. You can stop doing it and then start again. Each time you use the system, you lose weight and you feel better. You don't have to buy low-fat chemical substitutes for real food. There's no guilt, no calorie-counting and there are no forbidden foods. You don't need belief or willpower. You just use the system and listen to your body's signals.

Movement

Everyone agrees that you lose weight because you eat less and move more. This system creates the psychological environment in which you do that naturally without having to think about it. Naturally slim people don't need to go to the gym. On average they walk two thousand steps more than overweight people. Just two thousand extra steps are enough to speed up your metabolism. That is equivalent to a fifteen-minute walk.

You will find that you are moving your body more within one week of using this system, not because you have a regime or a workout programme, but simply because your body will prompt you to move a little more each day as you feel a natural desire to use and enjoy your muscles.

Because diets are unnatural they have to place a huge emphasis on willpower to constrict your eating and hit exercise targets. But you don't have to force yourself to go to the gym or take up a sport you don't like. Exercise is any movement of your body at all. Walking two minutes here and three minutes there, you can easily exceed fifteen minutes' walking a day without using any willpower, and your metabolism will speed up. When you are slim, using your muscles is a positively enjoyable experience. Even if right now the idea of 'exercise' is a complete turn-off, I promise you that within one month of starting this system, you will be looking forward to the stimulation and reward of physical movement.

Emotional eaters

There are many different types of emotional eater. Many used food as a comfort when they had difficulties or even trauma in their childhood. Some started using food to cope with stress. Some people who have survived abuse found that being overweight protected them from further abuse. There are different routes to emotional eating, and different emotional eaters have different relationships with their food.

- **Some have been dieters but have failed to keep the weight off in the long term.**

- **Some are happy with their actual weight but are continually stressed around food about maintaining that weight.**

- **Some eat healthily for three weeks and then go crazy for a week, and as a result carry more kilos than they want.**

All have discovered that whatever happens, they can rely on eating to make themselves feel better. Their biggest challenge is not food, or weight, but feelings. I first began to realize how significant this was many years ago when I met people who started using *I Can Make You Thin* but then just gave up – even some who had already started to lose weight!

As you will know if you've read any of my other books, I hate to be defeated. I have a particular personal crusade to offer the world a healthy, viable, honest alternative to what I believe to be the unhealthy, immoral and unsuccessful world of diets and diet clubs. So whenever anyone told me they had just given up, I questioned them very carefully.

One common theme emerged from all these different people. Deep down they believed that because they were emotional eaters, no system could work for them. They had accepted that being overweight was the price they paid for their way of dealing with their emotions. So any weight-loss system was going to be irrelevant. They believed the goal of losing weight was unattainable. They knew it wasn't about food or greed or being 'big-boned'. They just believed they had no alternative. Food was the only thing they knew that helped them to cope with their sensitivity to emotions.

If you recognize anything of yourself in these people, this book is for you. And this book is *particularly* for you if you believe it won't actually work. That is exactly the sort of belief that makes emotional eating appear such an unconquerable habit. And that is exactly what we will change.

No one is born an emotional eater. Emotional eating is a learned behaviour. And if you've learned to do it, you can unlearn it. I learned to drive in England on the left-hand side of the road. When I moved to the United States I didn't spend months learning to drive all over again. I got in the car and within a few minutes I adapted and picked up a new set of habits. With the help of this system, that's how quickly you can change.

As you overcome emotional eating, you will feel more in control because you will become a more emotionally intelligent person. Simultaneously you will increase your ability to relax. There will be moments that are challenging, but with all the tools in this system you will meet them successfully and learn from them. You will be able to transform potentially painful feelings from the past into emotional strength and intelligence for the present. You are going to lose weight and keep it off. At work you will become more effective and socially more at ease. You will replace eating with a far better way to feel better. And the better that you feel will be far, far better than before.

A happier healthier you

Food is part of the story. Weight loss is part of the story. But at heart this is all about you. This book is a guide to becoming a happier, healthier, better version of you. And unless you are underweight or already at your perfect body weight, the new you will be thinner and stay thinner for the rest of your life. But let's not run ahead. Let's start at the beginning. Right here, right now.

You are reading this because you want to stop emotional eating. That means one or more of the following is true for you:

- **You suppress and control your emotions with food.**
- **You are fed up with finding yourself eating food you don't want and don't need, for reasons you don't fully understand.**
- **You know there is a better way to eat and a better way to feel.**
- **You want to lose weight.**
- **You want to change the way you eat.**
- **You want to change your relationship with food.**
- **You want to maintain a healthy weight.**
- **Food helped you to get through bad times in the past, but you now want to find a better way to feel good.**
- **You can't face the misery and failure of yet another diet, but you really want a slimmer body and a happier life.**

All of this is going to change. *Freedom From Emotional Eating* will help you disentangle your emotions from your eating. I will show you new ways to eat and a new relationship with your feelings. The best way to eat is to enjoy every single mouthful of food you put in your mouth. That is the third of the Four Golden Rules from *I Can Make You Thin*. In Chapter Three I will briefly recap the Four Golden Rules because they are not just the royal road to weight loss, they also sum up a healthy and enjoyable relationship with food. Naturally slim people naturally follow the Four Golden Rules, and so will you.

However, the main focus of this book is a new relationship with your emotions. Maybe you only want to stop emotional eating in order to lose weight. If so, you are about to get a far better deal than you realized. You are about to release the true wisdom of your emotions, a whole new world of understanding of yourself and others. We can't control what happens in life, but we have a big say in how we respond and how we feel, and this system will give more control over your feelings.

Four strands

This isn't just a book, it's a system, and each element contributes to your success. The system has four parts.

First, the text explains the system and gives information to both your conscious and your unconscious mind. Knowing what is happening, and knowing that there is proper scientific research behind every element, will make it easier for both parts of your mind to make these changes.

Secondly, on the CD there is a Hypnotic Trance. The Trance is like having a personal session with me. Thousands of scientific studies have demonstrated that hypnosis is one of the most powerful and safe agents of psychological change, used by doctors and psychologists all over the world. The Trance will reprogram your unconscious mind, removing old habits and releasing your natural abilities to eat healthily and feel confident and at ease.

Thirdly, on the DVD I personally guide you through an amazing psychosensory process developed by my good friend Ronald Ruden. Dr Ruden has worked in this field for over a decade and with this development I believe he has cracked the code for personal change.

Fourthly, throughout the system there are short, simple techniques to guide you through weight loss and the complete range of emotional experience. I have developed them over years of working with a huge range of people from rock stars to royalty.

There is so much in this system that you may not take it all in consciously at first. That doesn't matter. The techniques are so powerful that just one or two of them are enough to get you off to a flying start. I frequently hear people quote a saying that it takes twenty-one days to change a habit. In my experience with hypnosis and psychosensory techniques, it can take just twenty-one minutes. I demonstrated the basis of this system on the *Dr Oz* show in the United States and worked with three ladies for less than half an hour. By the end of the week they had all lost weight. As you continue to use the DVD, the CD and the exercises, you will build up an unstoppable momentum for change that will transform your body and your life for the better.

Be as sceptical as you like

A few people have said to me, 'I used your system to try to prove you wrong, because I couldn't believe it would work. But it did. If you follow the instructions, it works.'

So if you are sceptical, carry on. Don't take anything for granted. Believe in this system only when you have the physical evidence from your own body and your own life that you can eat less, weigh less and feel better without missing out and without using food to control your feelings. Then you will not be reliant on beliefs or outside help or faith. Instead you will gain the confidence and sense of achievement you deserve because you have achieved success by your own actions and the power of your own unconscious mind.

All you have to do is follow the instructions and use the tools you are given, and you will give yourself the evidence that you can permanently improve your relationship with emotions and with food.

Lose weight

You will lose weight. It just so happens that you are going to get a bonus of a whole new approach to life too. And if that sounds a bit intense, don't worry, it will all happen gradually, one step at a time. That's kind of fitting, because the healthy way to lose weight is gradual as well. Your body gets slimmer and fitter little by little, day by day. In the same way your experiences become richer and you become more emotionally resilient each day.

Losing weight in a healthy way is a holistic readjustment of the whole of your body, your mind and your emotions. When you change one element, everything else is affected because it is part of one big system. So losing weight is a complex process of interactive changes. If you are looking at just one element of it – your weight – you will see that it does not reduce smoothly in regular, even steps. You can expect the actual weight loss to go faster and slower, to plateau, even occasionally to reverse, because it is just one element of a much bigger, more complex and subtle adjustment. Emotional freedom is also part of this process and, similarly, progress is neither linear nor regular. Some days feel like amazing breakthroughs. Other days it can feel like you are going sideways. Actually, throughout the process the whole of you is changing, but different elements are doing so at different speeds.

Success

The most unexpected challenge people meet as they make these changes is not fear of failure, but the reality of success. Things really are going to change with your eating, your food and your life, and the actual changes are relatively easy. Realizing that you have genuinely changed completely can be harder. As time passes, you are going to be getting used to a different idea of yourself.

I was working with a famous actress who struggled for years with eating disorders. She has always looked fabulous but she hadn't eaten normally for years, if ever. She relaxed and I took her into a hypnotic trance and I began to explain to her and to her unconscious mind the changes that were about to occur and how they would work. Suddenly she sat bolt upright and exclaimed, 'Hang on, this might actually work!'

She just looked at me for about thirty seconds and then lay back and went into a profound trance. About fifteen minutes later she woke up, and from that moment on she had no more problems with food. As you use this system, little by little your secret wishes will become possible. You will carry on making adjustments until you feel completely at home in your new way of life.

Changing habits easily

All human beings have at least three things in common: we all eat, we all have feelings and we all run on habits. This book will have a radical and positive effect on all three of these things. We are not going to start with food or feelings. We will start with habits. A habit is any process which has become automated and is wholly or largely run by the unconscious mind.

We use habits to tie our shoelaces, write notes and type letters. So, for example, you practised using a keyboard, and now you don't have to look for each letter one at a time. Habits help us deal with thousands of potential choices without having to think about all of them each and every day. Habits are wonderful, but the downside is that *even the process of creating habits is automatic.* Anything we do repeatedly can become a habit, even when we don't intend it to.

Emotional eating is a habit. It may be that once you were upset, and you chose sensibly to comfort yourself by eating something. If you occasionally eat a couple of cookies and you feel better, it is not going to have a significant effect on your life or your body. But if once in a while little by little becomes a regular fix, then, without any deliberate intention, you have built yourself a habit. And if the habit is triggered by more and more feelings, it becomes an automatic response to anything mildly disturbing. A reasonable action of being kind to yourself in a crisis turned into a habit that puts weight on your body and undermines your emotional intelligence.

Using the unconscious mind

How you eat and how you feel are complex, habit-driven behaviours which are fundamental to your existence. We need to eat. If we didn't eat, eventually we would die. We feel all day long, we can't stop feeling. So overcoming emotional eating is not as simple as stopping smoking. You need to eat and you need to feel, but just to do so in a different way. So we will change your habits around food and feeling.

We are not removing habits, but rather altering them. We take the start of a habit and give it a different ending, so we will take each of the triggers that used to lead to emotional eating and redirect them to a powerful new way to process your feelings.

You will do a lot of this with your conscious mind. However, we can make the whole process of change a lot easier and quicker by using the Trance to talk directly to the unconscious mind, which is the repository of all your habits, and also a resource of wisdom that is massively bigger than your conscious mind.

Many people think of consciousness as the core or centre of themselves, because it is constantly evident. It is our awareness. In fact, it is more like the tip of the iceberg. There is far more going on in the unconscious than we could ever fit into our conscious awareness. Your unconscious mind runs all your habits, it monitors all your sensory awareness and it runs the wonderful, complex system that keeps your heart beating, your lungs breathing and all the other functions going that keep you alive. However bright you are in your conscious mind, your unconscious mind is a thousand times cleverer. Later on in the book we will explore many other ways in which we can draw on the wisdom of the unconscious. But the easiest, most powerful way to start is to use the Hypnotic Trance that comes with this book.

Hypnotic Trance

The CD contains a Hypnotic Trance. You must listen to it only in a place where you can safely be unaware of the outside world and remain undisturbed for twenty minutes. Do not use it while driving or operating machinery.

Hypnosis is a natural process, like meditation. It doesn't matter whether you do or do not consciously remember the whole experience. Most people experience it as an extremely deep form of relaxation, and the more often you go into trance, the more profound the effect and experience.

This recording is like a personal session with me. Research has shown that recordings of hypnosis are just as effective as live sessions. In some ways they are better. It is like comparing a theatre show with a film. The advantage of the film is we can choose the very best takes and edit it to deliver exactly the response we wish. The design, the delivery and the recording of the Trance is aimed directly at your unconscious mind. Don't worry if you don't consciously hear every word or if you drift off as you are listening. Your unconscious mind hears and receives all it needs to start and sustain your liberation from emotional eating.

The suggestions in the Trance gradually reset your habits and reinforce your inner confidence and resilience. We are going to reprogram your unconscious to eat less and move your body more. Your unconscious mind will utilize the key suggestions in the right order for you. As everyone is different and we all have different histories, the rate of change and absorption varies from person to person, and the order in which changes happen will vary too.

Some of you will find that the first thing you notice is you are more relaxed; others will find that your appetite changes first, so you enjoy your food more. Others notice immediately that you eat less and feel better in your body. A few people will find that they are much more aware of their emotions, and notice that their body is helping them to relax and experience their emotions more deeply without the need for the comfort or distraction of food.

But however it starts, as you continue to listen to this Trance and use the system over a period of months, all the benefits of the Trance and of the work and exercises you do with your conscious mind will show up in your life.

I would like you to listen to this Trance every day for seven days. That is the absolute minimum. You can listen to it more often or for longer. Many people find that listening to the Trance every evening helps them to relax and follow the system effortlessly. After the first seven days, I strongly recommend that you use it at least once a week until you are totally used to your body feeling great, you are completely capable of facing all the challenges life throws at you, and you are enjoying your life to the full.

DO NOT LISTEN TO THE TRANCE WHILE DRIVING OR OPERATING MACHINERY.

If you suffer from epilepsy, please consult
your doctor before using this Trance.

If you can safely sit somewhere undisturbed for
about twenty minutes, listen to the Trance now.

If you cannot listen to it now, make time to listen to it
before the end of the day. One of the best times to listen
to it is in bed before you go to sleep.

CHAPTER TWO

•

How to Stop
Feeling Bad

How to stop feeling bad

Just before we totally eliminate emotional eating from your lifestyle, let's admit one thing: it helped you cope with overwhelming or difficult times, at least in the short term. And it is worth noticing two more things. The first is that you had a need to control how much you felt your emotions. The second is that with time emotional eating becomes less effective, so there was a tendency to eat more and more, chasing a moment of comfort that became increasingly elusive. We all know that taking a box of cereal or a tub of ice cream to bed at night is not healthy. One part of us just wants to do it, and another knows that the next morning we won't feel good about having eaten a litre of ice cream at midnight. But in the middle of the night it delivers a moment of comfort.

For some people, emotional eating happens so often that it becomes a habit of eating too much all the time. They do it again and again, getting more frustrated and feeling worse and worse about themselves. Then they get upset that they are overweight so they eat even more to suppress that feeling and it becomes a vicious circle. The emotional comfort just becomes a blur, the eating happens mindlessly.

But emotional eating is not just about controlling painful or uncomfortable feelings. Some emotional eaters automatically reach for the cookie jar whenever *any* emotion gets too powerful. They eat because they are happy or excited just as often as they eat because they are lonely or disappointed or bored.

Explaining emotional eating

I'm going to explain the science behind emotional eating and how we overcome it in an easy and straightforward way. As you read this section, the information is available to both the conscious and the unconscious parts of your mind. You may find it interesting at the conscious level, and it is also useful to your unconscious mind. The more your unconscious knows, the more swiftly and efficiently it can use the material you hear in the Trance. It will take all it needs to support the changes you are making.

Your unconscious is already beginning to build new ways of thinking and processing how you feel. You won't necessarily notice it happening but you will begin to react differently, and you will begin to feel so good on the inside that you won't want to change how you feel with food.

Emotional eating changes how we feel by several different mechanisms. The first is called displacement, and it is an effect of the natural limits of our consciousness. Famously, psychologist George Miller published a paper in the 1950s indicating that the maximum number of objects we can hold in our short-term memory is seven plus or minus two. Our awareness has similar limitations. We can only hold in consciousness a few ideas, perceptions and feelings at once. After a certain point, a new thought, sensation or emotion takes the place of an earlier one. Eating takes up a lot of our attention. Even just thinking about food takes up a lot of space in our minds. Some people wake up in the morning and begin planning their meals for the whole day. When we pay attention to what our food looks and smells and tastes and feels like it can be very absorbing, and in that way it just doesn't leave any room for other thoughts or feelings.

The second mechanism is simply the activity of eating. All the actions of eating are automated. All human beings use muscle memory. In other words, when we repeatedly practise a movement, like tying our shoelaces, it becomes automatic. We just have to start, and our muscles carry on. The same is true of eating. These actions of eating can be deeply familiar and comforting.

The chances are that if you are overweight, you eat fast and you are not even aware of it. The rate at which we eat is determined by muscle memory and our brain chemistry. This system changes your rate of eating. Two very well-known women who used this system decided to test my theory and one lunchtime had a slow-motion eating contest. They laughed as they cut up their food and brought it to their mouths like an action replay from a football match. However, they were amazed to notice that the next time they went to eat, they automatically ate more slowly and far less. Simply by playing this game once, they re-patterned their muscle memory.

Thirdly, eating physically interferes with how we register emotions. We have nerve endings in the solar plexus, where we register powerful emotions. Emotions originate from the brain, but can express themselves anywhere in the body. This is why, for example, when we are nervous we might say we have butterflies in the stomach. The solar plexus lies just above the stomach and intestines. When we eat, the sensations from the stomach and the small intestine overlie the signals from the solar plexus, making them appear less intense.

Last, and most important, eating releases serotonin, also known as the 'happy brain chemical'. When we do anything that reinforces our survival, such as eating, having sex or reaching a peak of achievement, we get a release of serotonin. Some people eat excessively because it delivers a serotonin high, even though it is a short-lived peak with significant long-term negative consequences.

Low serotonin

Some emotional eaters have a low background level of serotonin. Others are sensitive to particular contexts that drive down their serotonin. The contexts that people find stressful vary enormously. Some people experience stress at work and have a stash of food they use to manage their stress. Others thrive at work but hit a low moment when they go home in the evening, and immediately eat to change how they feel. Yet others are experiencing relationship difficulties or separations and look to food for comfort. And, of course, there are those who have eaten too much for whatever reason, but now find their own weight and ill-health stressful and eat to deal with that. We all have different reasons, but the chemistry is the same.

If you have discovered that eating makes you feel better, but that the 'better' feeling fades away after a while, there is a good chance that your serotonin levels are context-sensitive, or even too low overall. As you have discovered, emotional eating does raise your mood briefly, but the effect doesn't last.

What makes people vulnerable to low serotonin levels? Dr Ronald Ruden has been working in this area for many years and he believes that the major cause of chronic or repetitive low serotonin levels is one experience or more that causes a person to believe, 'I don't know how to solve this and I don't know when it is going to end.' It could be a single event or trauma, but most people have experienced one little disappointment or emotional pain after another until one day the thought goes through their mind, 'This hurts but I don't know what to do.' The body codes that as inescapable stress.

Under stress, the body lowers serotonin to free the mind to seek solutions so that we can deal with whatever is causing us stress. If you have low serotonin levels, it is not your fault, it is a result of stressful situations in the past. A huge range of situations can create this outcome and they are not all easy to recognize.

Low serotonin levels cause us to gravitate towards compensatory behaviour, such as emotional eating. The good news is that the system in this book teaches your body to raise your serotonin levels, so that whatever the situation, you remain in control.

Research

Dr Ruden's research suggests that if you experience a difficult time or trauma in which the stress appears inescapable, certain receptors on the amygdala, the part of the brain that controls our response to stress, are chemically changed so that the pathway of stress response is streamlined. In other words, your brain has become more sensitive to certain stimuli. Any stimulus that creates a situation similar to the one that was perceived as inescapable will trigger the same response.

The more often this happens, the more the brain makes associations to this state, shifting the neurochemistry of the brain to a low-serotonin landscape. In most cases, people have experienced many different incidents that have cumulated in an encoding that predisposes them to stress. Hence many different incidents and consequences can appear involved in the triggers for emotional eating. No wonder it can appear so baffling.

We like to think that if life is reasonably pleasant we should feel OK, in the same way that if we sit in a warm house we should be comfortably warm. However, when these pathways get encoded in the brain, often we don't feel OK because of the low-serotonin landscape. In such a state we seek out other ways to reduce the stress, and certain activities, including eating, will do so, even though only temporarily. That is like turning on a heater in the house, but leaving the front door open, so that as soon as we turn the heater off we feel the cold again.

Origins

There are many possible causes of this predisposition to low serotonin. One of the most common are events in childhood that impact on our self-esteem. For example, we may have failed an exam, broken something precious or simply been frightened. Every single one of us has had situations like this. If we receive the conscious love, encouragement and support necessary to keep us feeling genuinely safe, loved and loveable, there is no lasting damage. We live and learn. We discover that when we are loved we will survive our emotions, however strong they are.

If, on the other hand, it looked as though we could not escape the situation that troubled us, or no one was there to love us and help us at that time, a situation is created with all the ingredients to encode the event in the brain as a trauma, whether we are aware or not. If the situation is perpetuated and the feelings continue, any future contexts associated subconsciously with it will trigger low serotonin.

You can't necessarily tell from people's external circumstances how they feel inside or what their dominant serotonin levels will be. I worked recently with a wealthy high achiever who came from a very privileged background. His parents had a big house and everything money could buy. Then at seven years old he was sent off to a boarding school. Emotionally, he felt totally abandoned. That feeling of abandonment and loneliness stayed with him in spite of the wealth by which he was surrounded and all the success he later achieved. As a result, almost every time he was on his own he felt a terrible and crippling loneliness. In his relationships he had repeated fears about being left, which were not justified by reality. His fear and loneliness were magnified because the contexts triggered a low-serotonin level established in his childhood.

Context is key

The perception of inescapable stress causes the chemical landscape of the brain to change. Some people have serotonin levels that are lower than average. Others have a level that dips in particular contexts, such as being stressed, which reactivates the response to the original trauma.

Both cases shift people from a state in which feeling good is normal and feeling bad is exceptional to the exact opposite. Feeling bad becomes normal and feeling good requires a specific stimulus. Therefore, we develop all sorts of strategies to cope, but underneath them all the traumatized response remains. Even if we are no longer in a stressful environment, we are left with a chemical landscape in the brain with a tendency to revert to low serotonin whenever we are not actively lifted by environmental factors.

I worked with a lawyer who was desperate to lose weight. His practice was highly successful but also highly stressful. He would work from early in the morning to four in the afternoon without a break. Then all of a sudden he would hit a low serotonin point and feel completely out of control. He would order a giant pizza and eat the whole thing in seconds. The first thing I taught him was to change how he felt without using food. Then I taught him to pay attention to his body so he would notice if he was hungry before 4 p.m. Within days he had radically changed his timetable and his eating habits, and he lost weight effortlessly.

Vicious circles

It may be that we experience a situation in adult life in which the stress appears inescapable. This is not necessarily a single event. It could be being stuck in a loveless marriage, doing a job you hate or caring for a relative without help or holidays.

When people suffer from deep, permanent stress, they are very likely to seek relief. Some take to emotional eating, some to drink or drugs, others to shopping or extreme sports. All provide temporary relief. None addresses the underlying problem.

Unfortunately, the activity that provides temporary relief often creates further problems in the long term. Alcoholism, drug addiction and obesity all seriously threaten health and are thus in themselves inescapable stressors, creating more inescapable trauma and building an increasingly negative vicious circle. Some people end up using food alongside other addictions, which makes the problem appear even more complicated and intractable. Happily, Dr Ruden's work has shown there is a solution.

Escape

We all suffer difficult times at some point, whether in childhood or later on, although we may not be aware of it at the time. So how come some of us seem to survive without long-term damage, and others still seem to be vulnerable?

It seems that if we receive genuine loving comfort and we are distracted from the pain while the trauma or the memory of the trauma is still active, the encoding is not permanent. Our brains return to their natural resilient state.

Mothers do this for their children over and over again. The child gets frightened, the mother picks him or her up, hugs them and directs their attention to something else while continuing to hug and stroke them. This comforts them and they know they are safe and have escaped from danger. Without this immediate comforting, the brain may encode a stress. We are traumatized and the brain fixes the response. If a memory is reactivated, either by a similar stimulus or inadvertent thought, the child releases stress hormones.

Dr Ruden's research has shown that after reactivation of the encoded event, the physical actions of comforting, such as stroking the arms, face and hands, produce an electrical response of delta waves in the brain which strip away the chemical that was jamming the stress pathway open, thus returning the brain to its normal, pre-traumatized state. The actions of love are not just culturally significant gestures, they affect our physiology.

How trauma is encoded

Even today, with thousands of doctors and scientists around the world studying the brain, its actual mechanisms are still only partially understood. However, we do know quite a bit about a type of memory storage called synaptic memory, which is involved in encoding traumatic memories.

When something traumatic happens to us, we feel bad and we want to get away. In biological terms, data from our senses is fed to the amygdala, along with the data from the cortex, which ascribes meaning to the event. In the amygdala, neurons are activated, sending neurotransmitters to receptors on other neurons across the synaptic gap. In stressful situations, one particular neurochemical called glutamate is released, which is scooped up by a receptor known as the AMPA receptor, which passes the message on to release the fight or flight response. The AMPA receptor is then reabsorbed.

If the traumatic situation is perceived as inescapable, phosphorus is released, which glues the AMPA receptor to the surface of the neuron. This sets the pathway of the stress response permanently to open. So, if the event is merely recalled, the thought triggers a reaction as if the event was happening for the first time, repeating the stress response. Over time, repeated triggering of the stress response reduces the base level of serotonin.

Good news

The good news is that the mechanism to reset your brain's response remains available throughout your life. By treating the original, underlying cause, the driver for emotional eating can be removed. Even multiple causes and multiple problems can be cured by repeated, methodical treatment. Regardless of the cause, this system reduces the emotional overwhelm behind emotional eating and lets you process the emotions safely.

In a nutshell, this system delinks the thought from the feeling so you can remember whatever happened but the distress is removed.

Dr Ruden has also discovered that there are many ways in which we can become resilient and prevent traumas encoding permanently, regardless of the love and comfort we do or don't receive from the outside. At a physical level, yoga, meditation and exercise all increase resilience. Clear thinking, the ability to regulate emotional responses, optimism, an active problem-solving approach and moderation are all positively correlated with resilience.

At last there's an easy way

After years of research, Dr Ruden has devised a technique called Amygdala Depotentiation Therapy (ADT), otherwise known as 'Havening', which delinks the emotional aspect of the event so that we now view it as neutral and detached. This causes the brain to reset its landscape. He calls it Havening because it produces in the patient the experience of a safe haven, a place free from trauma. You will use Havening to depotentiate the receptors on the stress-related pathways in your brain and remove the underlying stress beneath your emotional eating. Research has shown that Havening is an extraordinarily powerful technique. Dr Ruden and I have successfully treated severe cases of post-traumatic stress disorder, war veterans and holocaust survivors. We have helped people who were overweight, and people who were depressed. Havening cures emotional overwhelm regardless of the initial cause of the problem.

The overwhelm is removed, but the memory and the understanding remain. As emotions no longer colour your perceptions, it is like have a filter removed. Instead of feeling overwhelmed, you can now see and assess situations clearly.

Havening is a huge breakthrough because it is so flexible. The Havening touch goes directly to the solution by causing a physiological change in the brain. It can be used even when a problem has multiple causes. It can be used across the whole range of psychological problems that generate emotional overwhelm. It delinks the traumatic response from the causative memory so, although you still remember whatever happened, you are no longer emotionally affected by it.

If you are interested in learning more about how Havening can be used in other areas of personal change, go to www.havening.org for details of all the latest research.

At the back of this book is a DVD in which I take you through the Havening process step by step. I'd like you to watch this DVD as soon as you reach the end of this chapter. This DVD is more than an instruction manual. It is like a personal session with me in which we haven all of the different drivers of your emotional eating.

Some people will remember specific incidents of inescapable stress from their past, others can simply work with more recent events that triggered their eating. It doesn't actually matter where you start, what does matter is that you simply follow the instructions. You can continue to use the DVD to treat each trigger or incident until you feel you are totally free of the need to indulge in emotional eating. You have reduced your level of background stress and restored your serotonin to a positive level. You will still retain all the memory and knowledge you gained from the incidents in your past, but they no longer depress the neurochemical landscape of your brain.

How Havening works

Havening works by evoking the memory of the initial trauma, which activates the neural pathway and the stress response described above. But then, instead of letting it run its course, we introduce the Havening touch, which floods the brain with delta waves (the same brain waves that are found in deep sleep). These delta waves cause the phosphorus molecule to release the AMPA receptor from the neuron's surface. The AMPA receptor is reabsorbed, thus delinking the stress response from the memory. Now the same stimulus can evoke the memory but doesn't generate the same stress response.

Unlike the temporary fixes of food, or other state changers such as drugs or alcohol, Havening makes you feel good *and* it cures the problem permanently.

When we started using Havening, we treated one trauma at a time. As we have refined the technique, we have found that it is in fact more powerful if we do it several times in succession, and if we allow the mind to group together responses to different traumas that have contributed to the same symptom.

This is an extraordinary breakthrough, because it allows us to heal entire categories of discomfort. For example, I have been able to work with individuals to address the anger and frustration arising from the failure of a marriage in a single twenty-minute session. Dr Ruden has worked with holocaust survivors whose trauma stems back to events seven decades ago. In this context we can reduce all the frustration and anger caused by years of unsuccessful dieting in just twenty minutes.

As well as removing the stress arising from a specific traumatic event, Havening also alleviates the stress arising from ongoing emotional states. Any recurrent painful emotion causes the brain to use the same neural pathways to trigger the stress response. We can use Havening on traumatic memories, long-term conditions and recurrent emotional trauma. We can even use it on associations that have quite randomly developed fear responses, such as phobias. In each case, it has the same effect. It delinks the stress response from the memory of the event.

Life

Life is rich and complicated and sometimes difficult. At times our emotional experience is like a roller-coaster. That is just how it is, whoever you are. What varies between people is the degree to which we are free to use our emotions, and the level of serotonin in the chemical landscape of the brain. By repeatedly using the Havening technique, you remove the hard-wiring to stress and hence raise overall serotonin levels.

In practical terms that means you become more resilient. You feel better and more capable, even when life is demanding. Challenging experiences really do become opportunities for personal growth. It is easier to feel inspired and to be inspiring to others. It becomes realistic to live up to the challenges of your talents. That doesn't mean being perfect and happy all day every day. It means being more happy more often and finding more opportunities to learn.

Use Havening now

I'd like you to stop reading now and watch the Havening DVD. You will have a full twenty-minute session with me.

We will address more than one event. We will use the process repeatedly to delink stress responses in any area of your life related to emotional eating.

You will see me demonstrate the Havening process and then I will ask you to do it together with me. It doesn't matter what you start with. Maybe you can remember a hundred traumatic incidents, maybe none at all. Maybe all you are aware of is a feeling. Maybe it is loneliness, or fear, or shame, or anger or just boredom. Maybe you don't even know why you find yourself eating. Whatever your personal situation, we will work with the specific situations and triggers that caused your emotional eating and, one by one, uncouple the stress response.

Use this DVD and complete this session every day for five days and you will transform your life. The technique is so rewarding I am sure you will want to continue to use it for years afterwards, and you can do so using the video or, after you have memorized the sequences, you can do it on your own.

Just in case you were thinking, 'Oh, I won't do this now, I'll just think about it', I want to emphasize that Havening is at the core of this process of change. I need you to take twenty minutes a day to use this DVD. If you can't find twenty minutes a day, I don't think I can help you – in fact,

I don't think anyone can. I have run countless seminars in which mothers tell me, 'I don't have time! I have to work, look after the kids, cook dinner …' I've heard it hundreds of times and I give more or less the same reply each time. 'So are there no thin mothers in the world? What are they doing that you are not doing? They are taking time to look after the most important person in the family – the mother. Find those twenty minutes for yourself and everything – seriously, everything – in the family will go better.'

I'd like you to commit right now to taking twenty minutes a day to helping yourself achieve your dreams.

Being slim, feeling really good, energized and loveable will become your natural state. Use the DVD every day for five days. Let's start right now!

Play the DVD now, provided you have somewhere private where you can watch it and follow my instructions.

If you cannot do this straight away, make time to watch the DVD somewhere you cannot be undisturbed before you go to sleep tonight.

CHAPTER THREE

•

Eat Less, Enjoy More

Eat less, enjoy more

The Hypnotic Trance has started the process of change in your unconscious mind and established the basis of safe, new ways to experience your emotions. Havening allows you to reduce stress to manageable levels. Whatever happens, you now have an easy, powerful method to process what you feel without using food to dampen down your emotions. So now it is safe to start altering your eating behaviour.

Just in case you haven't read my other books, I will now quickly recap the Four Golden Rules, which I first published in *I Can Make You Thin*. As you follow these rules, you will lose excess weight gradually and healthily until you reach a natural, slim, healthy body weight. Interestingly, it has often happened that if people who are underweight follow exactly the same rules they gain weight until they reach a natural, slim, healthy body weight. The point is the Golden Rules simply get you to follow your body's natural wisdom. Naturally thin people eat like this without thinking about it.

THE FOUR GOLDEN RULES

WHEN YOU ARE HUNGRY, **EAT!**

When your body is genuinely hungry, it gives you an unmistakeable feeling. If you are not sure whether or not you are hungry, you are not really hungry. Real physical hunger builds up gradually and is a clear signal in your belly. When you feel that, and it is clear and continuous, it means your body knows it needs food. So eat.

Physical hunger is worth waiting for. It means you can eat safe in the knowledge that your food is really necessary, so you can enjoy it to the full. And because your body really wants it, it tastes better too!

People on diets impose an arbitrary limit on their bodies. For a very small number of people, that limit will fit their own natural patterns, so for them it will work easily. They are the people who seem to diet effortlessly and have no trouble with it. They aren't actually better than the rest of us, it is just a lucky coincidence that the arbitrary limits of the diet happen to fit with their metabolism.

For everyone else, the arbitrary limit of a diet puts the body into 'survival mode'. That slows down the metabolism, so weight loss is slowed down and hunger increases. As soon as the dieter relaxes his or her vigilance, the body's cravings drive a search for extra food. So the weight goes back on.

Diet clubs tell their members to fight this with willpower, so, when they fail, and 84 per cent of them do, the members feel it is their fault for not having enough 'willpower'. The real problem isn't willpower. The problem is diets! When dieters eat again they are just responding to their panic-stricken bodies. No wonder they feel terrible – fear followed by panic followed by guilt!

This system is not a diet. It works with your body, and uses your natural drive for health to help you. In this context it is very important to tell the difference between real physical hunger and the triggers of emotional eating.

Real hunger comes on gradually. It is clear, persistent and physical. You feel it in your belly. It is entirely separate from contextual cues. It doesn't suddenly come on when you walk past a restaurant or a sweet shop. It is not a response to being upset, or to fear, embarrassment or anger. It is not an idea to distract you when you are bored and feel like doing something different. Real hunger is a simple physical feeling in your stomach.

If you are not sure why you want to eat, just pause for a moment. If, after a few minutes, you can still feel the real sensation of hunger in your belly, regardless of what you are thinking about, you are probably really hungry. If you are still not sure, wait a few minutes more.

If you really are hungry, you are definitely going to eat and enjoy it, so there is no harm in waiting a few minutes more just to make sure.

GOLDEN RULE 2

EAT WHAT YOUR BODY WANTS

Human beings evolved from the same basic stock as other animals and we share our operating systems with other mammals. Wild animals seek out the foods they need to get the right quantities of vitamins, minerals, salts, proteins, fats and carbohydrates. Their appetites, like ours, are instinctual, and vary according to the animals' requirements and the seasons. If they lack certain vitamins, they will seek out the plants or animals that contain them.

For example, before migrating, animals eat extra food and store it as fat to be used up when they are travelling. Animals that hibernate eat more as winter approaches and lay down a layer of fat to keep them going while they are asleep. They don't think about it, they just follow their instincts.

Our bodies have the same instincts, so they know what we need. We become aware of our needs through our tastes and preferences. Unfortunately for us, the situation is complicated by our clever, clever brains. It is a bit too easy to *think* we know what we want to eat instead of *feeling* what we want to eat. The problem is that thinking is very quick and we can let it override the slower, less articulate signals from our instincts.

If you pass a picture of a hamburger and suddenly think, 'Oh, I'm hungry,' that is a thought – a reaction of your brain to the associations evoked by that picture. Your body may not be hungry at all. You need to take a few moments to check what your body really wants. Do you really feel that genuine feeling of hunger in your belly?

Rule Two is very important. Eat what your body wants to eat. Don't eat what you think you should eat, or what other people want you to eat. Your body might want salad or it might want sticky toffee pudding. The important thing is to trust your body.

There are three ways in which overweight people typically break this rule. The first is that they let themselves be over-influenced by what other people think they should eat. Advertising fills their minds with pictures and ideas about food, and they respond by eating before checking whether their body is really, truly hungry.

The second is by following artificial diets. Dieting forces people to follow external rules. Dieters must eat only so many calories per day, only good foods not bad foods, only artificial food substitutes. All these rules ignore the best friend you will ever have – the wisdom of your own body. When you tune in to the wisdom of your body, you will eat less overall, you will find yourself eating differently and making healthy food choices, but you will do so in a way that completely suits your body and your own path to a healthy weight. If you drive a car from London to Birmingham, you can't just put your foot on the accelerator and drive at the average speed of a journey to Birmingham. You'll crash within the first few hundred metres. You have to drive your own personal journey in your own personal circumstances. It is the same with losing weight. You can't just follow a diet and demand that you lose so much per week. Your body knows best what you need and how to reach your healthy weight.

The third way overweight people break Rule Two is by emotional eating, using food for its side effects regardless of what nourishment their body actually needs. This book and system totally eliminate the need for emotional eating. As you learn new ways to use and process your emotions, you won't need to use food. But as a living human being, you do still have to eat! So, remember, eat what your body wants and you will feel completely satisfied.

GOLDEN RULE 3

EAT **CONSCIOUSLY**
AND ENJOY EVERY MOUTHFUL

The first part of Rule Three, the principle of conscious eating, has been investigated by more than a dozen scientific studies all around the world. All of them have shown that it reduces the amount people eat. But in my book, that on its own is not good enough. It is vitally important that you also enjoy every mouthful. The moment that any aspect of the eating is not fully enjoyable, stop eating.

When you focus your consciousness completely on the entire process of eating every single time you eat, three things happen. First, you eat less. As you need to take time to fully experience and enjoy your food, you eat more slowly. That means you approach your satiety point – the feeling of fullness – more slowly and you notice it more easily, so you stop eating sooner. You don't suffer from the problem of overshooting it, which happens to people who eat quickly and without paying attention.

Secondly, you make new food choices. As you have raised your awareness of your response to food, you will find that your tastes change and you gravitate towards foods with a greater variety of flavours and textures. People who eat swiftly and unconsciously tend to eat foods that are high in fat, sugar and salt because the tastes are so brash and bold that they are noticeable in spite of being given little attention. When you really focus on your food, pure fat, sugar and salt begin to feel overwhelming or crude. You start trying different stuff.

Thirdly, you enjoy your food more. Instead of noticing it intermittently and being distracted, you focus on it and get more out of it. When you hear a bit of music behind the conversation in a crowded café, you can't really enjoy it as much as when you are at a concert where everyone is listening. With food it is the same: the more you pay attention, the more you enjoy. When you follow Rule Three properly, the whole experience of eating becomes far more enjoyable.

To follow Rule Three properly you must do two things:

1. **When you eat, focus all your attention on eating. Don't do anything else. Don't watch TV, read a book, browse the net, drink alcohol, solve crossword puzzles, drive a car, walk down the street or make phone calls. When you eat, just eat and NOTHING ELSE.**

2. **Eat slowly. Almost all of us have developed a habit of eating too fast. It is important to slow right down. Chew each mouthful of food twenty times – yes, twenty times. Use that time to savour it like a gourmet and enjoy the texture and flavours of your food to the full.**

Eating slowly helps you enjoy your food properly. If you aren't enjoying it, then you probably aren't hungry or you are eating the wrong food. In either case, stop eating. When you have stopped, pause for a while and let your body tell you what, if anything, it really wants. Eating slowly and consciously and enjoying every mouthful will vastly increase your pleasure so you will never feel you are missing out.

When you eat, sit down at a table and eat from a plate. Use a knife and fork and relish every moment. You can enjoy eating a meal with family or friends but don't talk and eat simultaneously. When you pick up a mouthful of food, pause and really notice everything about how it feels and tastes. That naturally will slow down your eating and reinforce the habit of eating slowly.

It may seem strange that I am making such a big deal of this. After all, it is not as if people are totally unaware of eating. We have to be conscious to open the fridge or a can of beans. Nonetheless, the body is so good at automating processes that it is very common for people to eat using only a very small part of their consciousness while the rest is doing something else. That habit of unconscious eating is how people lose track of their body's natural weight-control system in the first place.

Rule Three breaks the habit of unconsciousness. Eating consciously and enjoying your food resets your relationship to food. It respects the wisdom of your body, and lets you hear the signals it is sending you about what you really need to eat and how much.

That's why it is so important not to watch television, read, surf the net, phone, drive, stroll, write or text while eating. Always sit down and pay attention to your food, even if you are just having a snack or a bar of chocolate.

I remember working once with a woman who claimed she couldn't stop eating chocolate. I asked her to bring a chocolate bar to our session. I asked her to eat it in front of me and pay complete attention to the whole of the experience. She found herself eating extremely slowly, and halfway through she decided she had had enough. She must have eaten hundreds of those bars in the past, but this was the first time she had really noticed everything about it. She liked it, but she didn't actually want to finish it.

GOLDEN RULE 4

WHEN YOU **THINK** YOU ARE FULL, **STOP** EATING!

The feeling of fullness, or to use the correct biological term, 'satiety', is your body's natural signal that you've had enough food. Emotional eating is not driven by hunger or satiety, it is just an activity to mask emotions. Therefore, it causes people to ignore those signals.

As you no longer do emotional eating, you need to reconnect to all the natural signals of your body. Following Golden Rule Three makes it easier to follow Golden Rule Four, because slowing down your eating gives you more time to notice feeling full.

People ignore the satiety signal for lots of different reasons. If they are stressed or distracted or eating on auto-pilot, they can easily miss it. If they are eating just to change how they feel, they may not even have been hungry in the first place, so they will have eaten straight past it with the very first mouthful.

People who routinely overeat may have completely forgotten what that signal feels like because they are so used to ignoring it. Those people don't stop until they feel stuffed or uncomfortable or have a pain in the stomach.

The feeling of satiety is so important that the body has three separate ways of signalling it to the brain. The first is that levels of a hormone in the bloodstream called pancreatic peptide YY (known as PYY) increase as you eat. PYY tells your brain to reduce your appetite and also increases the efficiency of the absorption of nutrients in your intestines. In other words, the same process that makes sure you are well fed reduces your desire for food.

The second signal is a neuropeptide called Glucagon-Like Peptide-1 (known as GLP1), which is released into the bloodstream as food enters your intestines. GLP1 does many useful things for you, including promoting the feeling of satiety.

Alongside these two neurochemicals, the nerve endings in your stomach wall react as it is stretched and tell your brain that you have had enough to eat. So the body tells your brain to stop eating through a measure of the physical bulk of your food.

As there are three different ways to tell us when we have had enough food, it is clearly very important. Research has demonstrated this in the most stark way possible. Obesity strongly correlates with ill-health and early death. Eating well but not too much is highly correlated with a long and healthy life.

In the cities of the modern, developed world, we are continually presented with more food and more opportunities to eat than we could possibly need, so knowing when to stop eating is a vital skill. If we don't re-learn this skill, we are literally killing ourselves with too much food.

Stop eating as soon as you even think you are full. Wait a few minutes. If you genuinely feel hungry again after five minutes, then eat. If not, don't. It really is that simple.

The most natural way to eat

The principle throughout all the Golden Rules is the same: trust the wisdom of your body. You do that by paying close attention to its signals. When you are hungry, eat. Eat what your body wants: it will guide you through taste preferences. When eating, pay attention to what you are doing and how your body reacts and ensure you really enjoy it. Then when you get the signal from your body, just stop. All four rules are different aspects of helping you to get away from ideas about food and pay more attention to what your body is telling you it really needs.

The Four Golden Rules are the most natural way to eat. It is how animals in the wild eat. We are just learning to trust our instincts again. I would like you to follow them deliberately every single day, and in a little while they will become habitual. And because they are essentially the body's natural way of eating, it will become easier and easier and more and more enjoyable to follow them, and your body will feel better and better. Your digestion will begin to work better and you will feel more energized and more relaxed from the tip of your toes to the top of your head. And that in turn will mean you feel stronger and more fully resourced to experience your emotions differently and learn from them.

Eating patterns

Emotional eating is by definition unrelated to the real nutritional needs of your body. It has caused you to eat food you don't need at times when your body didn't need it. That affected your appetite and the chances are that your digestion has been disrupted too. So, for example, you may have gone for ages without properly feeling hungry. Or you suddenly feel ravenous, then, when you eat a snack, you feel over-full. You may have lost track of normal mealtimes.

The body is naturally rhythmical and works best when it has a regular eating pattern of a gradual build-up of genuine hunger followed by a good meal. It is difficult to maintain a healthy eating pattern when extra food is introduced randomly into the system. We can tell, from all the overweight people around, that a great deal of food is eaten when people aren't hungry. When eating patterns are irregular, people are more likely to eat snacks, adding to the body's confusion.

I suggest, therefore, that you do a little experiment and find out if you can discover a routine for eating that suits your body. There are many different ways to eat well. It could be three meals a day, but it doesn't have to be. For example, some people eat little and often, others eat one big meal and one small one. The key, as we know from the Four Golden Rules, is to eat when you are hungry, to eat what your body genuinely wants to eat, to eat consciously, and to stop when you feel full. See if you can create a routine that helps you do that.

Strangely, although we have more choices, more types of food and more restaurants and other food outlets than ever, it is more and more difficult to eat well in the modern world. There are too many choices, and far too many businesses trying to get past the natural limits of your system of hunger and satiety by stimulating your imagination with pictures and ideas about food.

Our own system of signalling a genuine need for food is simple and, unless you are absolutely starving, it is quite low key. We can easily survive all day without food. But we are surrounded by advertising, restaurants, street food, shops and takeaways all constantly trying to sell food to us. Following the Four Golden Rules helps you to take charge of your eating again, and stops you being a victim of corporate advertising.

Lifestyle changes mean that it is unusual for a family to sit down and eat together at the same time every day. More and more people live on their own and eat out frequently. Many people fit their eating around a busy schedule of work, study, leisure and family commitments, so the time of day at which they eat is constantly being shifted. I meet mums at my seminars who make a real effort to ensure their children eat regular, healthy meals but never actually get to sit down, relax and eat properly themselves. Often they just snack from their children's plates. Their children are well nourished but their own diets and weight suffer.

As you follow this programme you may well eat less than before, but you will give it more importance in your life. When every single mouthful is enjoyable, it is worth rearranging other parts of your life to make enough time to sit down regularly to fully appreciate your meals.

Overcoming delusion

I doubt if anything I have written in the section above is really news to you. We all know that what people eat and how they eat has changed a lot. We all know about lifestyle changes and the increase in obesity in the developed world. However, one curious thing I have noticed from the hundreds of thousands of people I've worked with is that many people who are overweight like to behave as though it is a bit of an accident. They like to imagine that the excess food they eat is not that important, or that it is really only every now and then that they have an extra snack. Mostly there is an unconscious, and therefore unchosen, pattern to their extra eating.

In particular, people have a tendency to minimize the amount of emotional eating they do for a very simple reason. Emotional eating means eating to diminish, disguise or cope with challenging emotions. Because we are trying to avoid those emotions, we don't want to pay too much attention to the means by which we do so in case it draws attention to why we are doing it in the first place. We prefer to delude ourselves. This system makes it safe to give up that delusion.

Simple

Life gets a lot simpler when you trust your body. You discover you are free from the endless worrying about food. No more counting calories or wondering if this thing really counts or how many calories there are in a smoothie. No more long discussions in your head about whether or not to eat a cake, or order a pudding or buy some fruit. If you are really hungry, listen and discover what your body really wants, then eat it. Eat slowly. When you are full, stop. If you are not hungry, no worries. Simple.

Not so simple

That sounds great, doesn't it? What could go wrong? Well, I discovered as I worked with people following the Four Golden Rules that what went wrong was that many of them had well-established habits of eating without thinking. They had done it for so long that when they tried to pay attention to their food, if their concentration slipped for a second, the old habits took over and they found they had eaten whatever was on their plate with no awareness whatever.

These people were very willing and well intentioned, but they found themselves falling into old patterns of unconscious eating in spite of their conscious efforts. They needed more help and from a different place. That is why I created the 'Listen While You Eat' recording.

I would like you to use the 'Listen While You Eat' track of the CD at least once a day when you sit down to eat. It will remind you of the Four Golden Rules precisely when you need them and it includes some other helpful messages too.

More help

I am continually looking for ways to make positive personal change easier and more efficient. I like to keep track of the latest research and I am looking for what works, regardless of how it works.

Recently I found a study that seemed at first to be quite extraordinary. Psychologists have discovered that people who prayed before they ate consumed less food. Prayer helped them lose weight.

I am very much of the opinion that a person's religion – or lack of it – is their own business and not mine. But this intrigued me. Did faith help people lose weight? Did believing in God make you thinner? The answer was no. The study did not assess or explore people's faith or beliefs. It did not matter whether people believed in God or which religion they did or did not belong to. The reduction in eating was correlated to the action of prayer.

The very word 'prayer' conjures up religion for many people, and many of us have very negative associations with religion. In fact, I have quite a few friends who passionately believe in God and equally passionately hate religion. As a result of my own experiences at school, I used to be attached to an extremely negative view of Catholicism. Nowadays I still remember with sadness the injustices I saw and experienced, but I am no longer troubled by them. I know that each of us has to find our own path through life.

At the most basic level, prayer is asking for help from some source other than your own conscious mind. People pray to different gods, to saints, to gurus, to stars, stones or ancestors. Whoever or whatever they pray to, the request is the same: please do something extra to help me, beyond what I can achieve on my own.

Do what works

I looked at the study on prayer and experimented with its basic structure, which is asking for help from something other than your conscious mind. I discovered that it works *even if you don't know whom or what you addressing.* Some religions believe that all of us have a spark of the divine within. Maybe there really is a link between some of the activity in our brains that we don't yet understand and a greater supra-human force. Personally I have to say I still don't know, but I do know the unconscious mind is very powerful.

If, before you eat, you ask for help from someone or something beyond your conscious self to eat consciously, enjoy your food and stop when you are no longer hungry, you will be more successful. So I invite you to do this from now on. Every time you eat, just before you put anything in your mouth, ask for help to eat mindfully from someone or something beyond your conscious self.

As you get used to doing this, you will gradually receive the help you ask for. That in turn helps you relax, which helps you eat more slowly, which helps you enjoy your food more and stop eating as you feel full and truly satisfied. You are reinforcing a virtuous circle of having more fun and having a healthy, slim body!

> **Use the 'Listen While You Eat' track**
> **for at least one meal a day**
> **for at least one week.**
>
> **Use it as often as you wish thereafter.**

Success Tracker: food

Psychological research has demonstrated that what gets measured gets done. It is also empowering to be able to look back at a record of your activities and see how much progress you have made. So I would like you to use the Success Tracker at the back of this book to keep track of using the Four Golden Rules.

> **Write in the Success Tracker each day for the next twenty-eight days.**

CHAPTER FOUR

•

Emotional Freedom

Emotional freedom

By the end of this chapter you will have a completely new way of understanding your feelings and you will be able to transform any feeling, however confusing, difficult or challenging, into a positive force in your life. If you are feeling sceptical or you've been depressed or you feel life has treated you harshly, you may find that difficult to believe. Just bear with me and read on.

I'd like to start by showing you a very powerful exercise I have used for many years, which brings your attention quickly into your body. Whatever is happening, whatever you are feeling, it is a way of pausing and refreshing yourself.

This exercise feels great, but it also has a particular use in this context. It allows you to slow down your emotional experience and make sense of what you are feeling. If you have emotions that have been suppressed by emotional eating, at first it can be difficult to untangle them.

This exercise also clarifies your attention and slows down your emotions so that you can sort them out one at a time. In this way it gives you a completely secure basis for positive emotional change.

Finally, this exercise is very simple, and you can do it almost anywhere. You can do it sitting quietly at home, or you can do it on a noisy bus or on a train or in a waiting room. None of the other passengers will even be able to tell that you are doing it.

Some people find they can do this easily after a single reading. Others prefer to have me guide them through it, so I have put it on the CD and you can listen to it there. For now, read the instructions so you know what to expect, then put on the CD, relax and let me help you.

INSTANT CALM

This is a super-simple but refreshing and centring exercise. Practise it every day for a week so that you know it off by heart and can do it whenever you want. You will find from time to time that when you feel an unexpected emotion or an impulse towards emotional eating, this exercise is a more rewarding and refreshing option.

1. Sit on a chair with your feet flat on the floor.

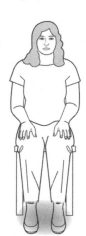

2. Pay attention to your feet. Notice the feeling of your shoes, socks or whatever you are wearing. Feel your heel and the ball of your foot on the floor. Notice what you feel in your toes. Feel the whole of both feet.

3. Now, saying the number '1' to yourself in your head, take a slightly deeper in-breath and pull that awareness up to your knees. Notice your ankles and shins and calves and all the way up to your knees so you are aware of the whole of your lower legs. Carry on breathing normally.

4. When you are ready, say the number '2' to yourself and with a slightly deeper in-breath pull your awareness up to your waist, so that you can feel all of your legs and your thighs and bum resting on the chair. Carry on breathing normally. Your awareness may come up the skin and soak inwards or up the bones and spread outwards. Either way is fine.

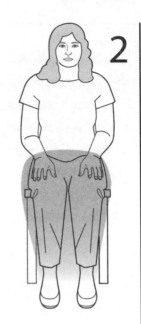

5. Next, say the number '3' to yourself and with a slightly deeper in-breath pull that awareness up to your shoulders. You may be more aware of one part of you than another. That's fine. Just let your awareness soak through the whole of your body. Carry on breathing normally.

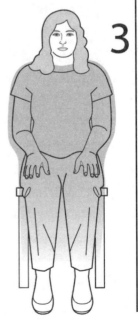

6. Next, with the number '4' and another in-breath, pull that awareness up from your neck over your chin, your cheeks, your ears and your eyebrows to the very top of your head. Carry on breathing normally and notice this gentle, overall feeling in the whole of your body. You may feel tension or emotions in some places – just let your awareness spread through those places and continue through every part of you.

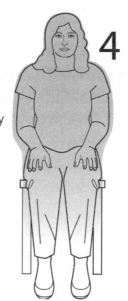

7. Then, with the number '5' and this time a slightly deeper out-breath, double your awareness down from the top of your head to your shoulders. Let it pass over your forehead, through your head, over your face and down your neck to your shoulders.

8. Next, with the number '6', and again a deeper out-breath, double it down to your waist, running like a ripple through your torso, along your arms to your fingertips and down to your waist. Carry on breathing normally.

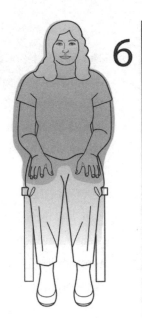

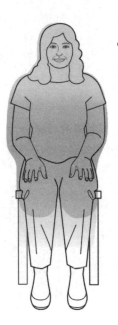

9. With the number '7', and again a deeper out-breath, double it down to your knees, soaking through your thighs to your knees.

10. Finally, with the number '8', and again a deeper out-breath, double it down to your feet, through your shins, calves, ankles and toes to the soles of your feet.

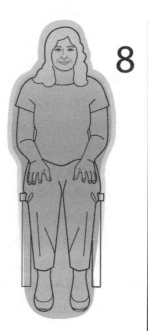

11. Sit there for a little while and notice the feeling of the whole of your body, just as it is.

When you are ready, if your eyes have closed open them, and reorient yourself to the world around you, refreshed, relaxed and alert.

Feel better

I'm going to show you how to feel better, how to be more at ease with your emotions and how to use them to enrich your life. By restructuring your own use of your emotions, you will transform your relationship to life, so that whatever is happening, your emotions become a guide towards fulfilment both in the outside world and in the inner world of your feelings and relationships. The most underdeveloped territory on Earth is not the Amazon nor the Antarctic nor the deep ocean floor. It is the human heart. Your emotions are the pathways to the new territories of your heart.

That sounds great, doesn't it? Except it probably doesn't sound much like real life. For most of us, most of the time, emotions don't seem anything like as exciting or rewarding as that. We're up, we're down, we're bored, we have a bit of fun. We go back to work. That's what it's like, isn't it? Well, maybe it is … but it can be a lot more fulfilling. And strange as it may seem, the route towards that greater fulfilment is directly through the feelings that we think we don't want.

Emotions

What are emotions? At the simplest level they are signals or messages. Fear protects you. It stops you from trying to walk across a busy road until the traffic stops. Desire motivates you, for example, by prompting you to ask for what you want. Anger defends you. If your standards are violated it fills you with the energy to stand up for yourself and what you believe in. Joy rewards you. When you achieve your desires, joy lets you relish what you have achieved, and when you are peaceful it lets you appreciate what life gives you.

However, there is more to emotions than these messages. Emotions are part of our intelligence. Emotions arise as our experience touches our own most personal needs, values and beliefs. In a sense they are the most fundamental part of our lives, because they reveal and reflect what we value most. When we are working properly with our emotions, they guide us further to develop those values and to fulfil our deepest ambitions. If we examine our emotions we can easily discover a rich world of meaning. Let me show you what I mean.

'Everything'

I was working with a woman who was depressed and overweight. I asked her to take some time to pay attention to how she was feeling.

'Oh no,' she said, 'I don't want to do that. I've been there too often before, that's why I'm always eating.'

It took some persuading to get her to agree.

Eventually she said, 'OK, I know what I'm feeling. I'm feeling bad.'

I asked her what sort of bad.

'Just bad,' she replied.

I asked her to try to be more specific. Was there a particular emotion she could name?

'Depressed,' she said.

'Do you know what makes you depressed?' I asked.

'Everything.'

'What is it about everything that is depressing?'

'Just everything.'

'OK,' I said, 'I'm looking at my bit of everything and I like it. What is it about your bit of everything that is depressing?'

'There's nothing to do.'

'So you would like to have something to do ...'

'Yeah, but I don't know what to do. I feel I haven't achieved anything and it is too late to start now.'

'So you would like to achieve something, too ... What would you like to achieve?'

'I just want to be happy.'

'And what sort of achievement would make you happy?'

'Well, it would be a start if I could hold down a relationship.'

'Would that make you happy?'

'Sure it would make me happy!'

'Great! So, please can you give me an example of a specific thing that would happen in that relationship which would make you happy?'

'I'd like to go to a restaurant with my own boyfriend and have him paying me attention so I felt good about myself.'

'OK,' I said, 'let me see if I can sum this up. You would like to achieve something. That could include spending time with a man who paid attention to you. And that means you would like to have some company and you would like to feel good about yourself. I'm sure you may want many other things, too, but is what I've said true?'

'Yes, it is,' she said.

'Right,' I said, 'from right here, right now, what is the smallest recognizable action you can take that moves you in the direction of any of those things?'

After quite a bit more discussion she decided to meet a friend for lunch. It wasn't a boyfriend, but it was a step towards it because it got her out of the house and meeting someone.

When I met her later that week, she looked much more upbeat and energetic. I asked her how her lunch went.

'Oh, it was great,' she replied. 'My friend had her laptop with her so we created a profile on a dating site and I've got a date at the weekend.'

Things don't necessarily move that fast for everyone, but the story shows what happened to that woman when she listened to her feeling and acted on its positive intention.

A new approach

Many people are not used to looking at their more challenging emotions in this way. Most of us tend to think we want more of the emotions that feel nice and we want to avoid the ones that feel uncomfortable. That seems like common sense, but there is a subtle problem. Because we don't want to pay attention to the uncomfortable feelings, we sometimes fail to get the message.

It is a bit like this. Imagine you are the boss of a big business and all day long people bring you messages. Good news comes in a gold envelope and bad news comes in a black envelope. At first half the envelopes you get are gold and half are black. You like gold ones, so you open them and reply to them. You don't like the black envelopes so you send them back again. After a while you get more and more black envelopes because the same ones get redelivered, and more things go wrong because you hadn't read the earlier messages, and you get fewer gold envelopes. If we reject the envelopes because of their colour, we fail to get half the messages from our emotions. You can see where this is going – it's not about the envelopes, it's about what's inside. If we don't get the messages from our uncomfortable emotions, we miss out on their guidance and intelligence.

We don't need to look for 'good' emotions or avoid 'bad' emotions. When we learn from all our emotions they will guide us naturally to a richer and more fulfilling life.

Understanding emotions

Very often when people come to see me because they feel bad, they feel confused and trapped too. They don't like what is going on, but they don't know where to turn.

I have found there are five questions we can ask which have a miraculous effect. It is not essential that people answer them all perfectly or even correctly. All they have to do is make an honest effort towards it. Sometimes I have asked people to guess the answer at first, and we have worked with that. In a little while we find out if their guess was accurate or close and we get enough information to carry on.

FIVE QUESTIONS

If ever you have an emotion which seems challenging in any way, ask yourself these Five Questions. These questions work with any emotions at all – whether enjoyable or uncomfortable – but people mainly use them with the painful ones because they want to change them. If it is a very painful emotion, you can slow things down with the Instant Calm exercise on page 101.

Just ask the questions and answer as best you can. Sometimes the answers seem totally obvious, sometimes they seem utterly baffling. In the end, it turns out that doesn't matter. We just try to answer them as best we can at the time, and as more is revealed, we answer them better and better. Here they are:

1. What is the *trigger* of this emotion?

2. What is the *belief or judgement* included in this emotion?

3. What is the *need or care* beneath this emotion?

4. What is the *positive intention* behind this emotion?

5. What is the *first practical action* I can take now to fulfil the positive intention?

How it works

Let me illustrate how this works with a very simple example. I'm sitting writing in a café and a bus stops outside. The engine keeps running and it's loud. I feel annoyed. I ask the Five Questions.

Q 1.   What is the trigger?

A 1.   *The emotion is a response to the noise.*

Q 2.   What is the belief or judgement?

A 2.   *I believe the noise is unpleasant.*

Q 3.   What is my need?

A 3.   *I have a need for a level of quietness to concentrate on my writing.*

Q 4.   What is the positive intention behind this emotion?

A 4.   *The positive intention of the annoyance is to re-establish the level of quietness I desire.*

Q 5.   What is the first practical action I can take?

A 5.   *I can move to another café – or I could ask the bus driver to turn off his engine.*

This sort of thing is so ordinary that you have probably done a version of it a thousand times in your life, but you didn't need to work through each question, you probably jumped straight to answer number five. The key is to realize that however baffling or uncomfortable an emotion may seem, we can ask these same Five Questions and use them to unfold the meaning of the emotion, even if it is as dull and apparently meaningless as 'I feel bad.'

If you look back at the conversation with the woman who was overweight and depressed earlier in the chapter, you can see that, in one form or another, all five questions are in that conversation. Sometimes we have to ask ourselves the questions several times before the answers become clear, but if you keep going you will get the answers you need.

Here's another example. One beautiful sunny morning I'm driving down the road and I think to myself what a lovely day it is, but then I notice I feel a tension in my solar plexus. There is nothing around me to cause it. I ask the Five Questions and recognize that I left home in a hurry and my girlfriend was trying to talk to me, but I didn't really give her my attention. Now this tension is in my body because I have a belief or judgement that I should have taken time to listen to her. What is the need underneath this emotion? It is my need for a loving relationship, and the positive intention is to protect that relationship. The practical action I can take is to make time to listen to her. The tension reminds me what I value. When I decide to make time for her, the tension fades away.

Just ask

In almost all of our lives we feel our emotions and act on them so swiftly that we don't notice how brilliantly they work for us. Just occasionally, however, they are baffling or painful. That's when we think emotions are a problem. In fact, they are still working for us, but either we don't understand them, or they include a belief or judgement that is out of date. In these situations, the Five Questions help us to understand and use our emotions. When we feel an emotion strongly, it is easy to believe we know the answer already, but that's exactly when we need to check. We can't tell in advance which question will prove most useful, so get used to asking all five – you never know which one will be helpful.

Sometimes it seems that we can't answer question one. We can't find what triggered or provoked a feeling, we just feel it. Other times the trigger doesn't seem to make sense.

If you can't answer question one or the answer doesn't make sense, there is a very strong chance that the emotion you are experiencing actually belongs to the past. Now that you have stopped emotional eating, little by little echoes of the emotions that were squashed are being released, and as you process each one you will feel better and better.

If you don't know the answer to question one, just carry on and try to answer the other questions. If you are not sure, just try your best guess. You don't have to get it all right instantly. As you have a go at working out the positive intention and the practical action to achieve it, you are likely to realize a bit more about the feeling as it changes in response to your action. All you need to do is do your best and run through the Five Questions over and over again, and little by little, one by one, the emotions you reveal will deliver their messages and guide you towards your own personal fulfilment.

Do you still agree?

Emotions can be confusing and even unhelpful when the belief or judgement they include is false or out of date. The second question allows us to check if we still agree with the belief inside the emotion. Here's an example. I worked with a man who told me he always avoided asking out women he found truly attractive. He got on very well with women, but the moment he thought about asking them out, he was overcome with shyness. It was clear the trigger for shyness was thinking about asking them out. I asked him the second question, what is the belief included in the emotion. The belief was that he would be very embarrassed. That is another emotion. So I asked what was the belief included in the embarrassment. He found that a bit more difficult to answer, but then he realized that the belief was that if he was rejected, the pain would be unbearable. I asked him if that was true today. The answer was no. He was braver than he thought. The belief inside his emotion dated from way back when he was a child. Now that he asked himself the question as an adult, he realized he had gained a lot of confidence since then and he was no longer so bothered. The question allowed him to update his feelings. I asked him how he felt about asking a woman out now. 'A bit nervous,' he said, 'but in a good way.'

His belief was out of date. As soon as he realized that, it faded away. Other times we find that beliefs include some expectation of ourselves. There's a very useful hint I can give you here. Look out for the words 'should' or 'ought'. Very often the judgement includes these words – as in 'I should be grateful' or 'I ought to have known that'. Every 'should' and every 'ought' refers to a rule, a standard or an authority which exists somewhere outside of you. It is worth checking very, very carefully whether you still feel you agree with that rule, standard or authority. Sometimes you don't. And when you don't agree with it, a new emotion based in your heart is free to emerge.

Unfolding emotions

Through our emotions we make sense of the world. That doesn't mean that everything we feel is a brilliant insight. It doesn't even mean we always get it right. Sometimes emotions are revelatory, sometimes they are misleading, but they are always meaningful. Sometimes emotions are based on judgements that don't even belong to us. For example, many of us have feelings based on beliefs we have unconsciously inherited from our parents. When we ask the Five Questions, those beliefs or judgements are revealed, and because we have brought them to consciousness we can examine them. If we realize we no longer agree with the beliefs and judgements that were buried inside our emotions, we are able to let them go.

I like to think of each emotion as a bundle of meaning that needs to be unfolded. By asking the Five Questions, you unfold the meaning one layer at a time. However complicated emotions may appear, there is always a route to clarity. Sometimes, such as in the case of shyness, when the belief or judgement is revealed, we find there is another emotion behind it to unfold. Sometimes that happens over and over again, until we reach a place of calm and understanding.

Processing our emotions makes us whole

As we develop our emotional abilities, we understand ourselves and the world better. Just as we can learn how to think better, so we can learn how to feel better. Our emotions are like another sense: by paying close attention to them, we sense and understand the world around us more deeply.

More than that, our emotions lead us into a deeper understanding of ourselves. As we unfold each emotion, it changes and shows us something new. As we grasp it, each emotion leaves a little residue of understanding that changes us and life becomes richer.

If we ignore an emotion it will keep coming back until we pay attention to it. This doesn't mean I have to be controlled by my emotions. It means I have to give them my attention. For example, once I decided to help a friend with a new business. It was a good idea, and I thought it would be successful. I felt a bit of fear about it, but I brushed it aside. I wanted to focus on success, not fear. The business took up a lot of my time and attention, but didn't succeed. Looking back, I realize my fear had a message. I thought the business was a good idea, but I was not passionate about it. My fear was trying to protect me, because at the emotional level my judgement was that I didn't care about it enough.

Each new emotional understanding also affects and develops our values. We see this in children as they gradually move from meeting their own needs to learning to value the love and friendship of others. As we move into adulthood, the emotional education carries on. And the more we learn from our emotions, the greater the wisdom and guidance they can bring us for future decision-making.

Reality check

About now you could well be thinking, 'Hang on, if emotions are great, helpful messages which put us in touch with our true self and help us to grow into our full potential, why do so many of us spend so much time avoiding them? And why are so many of them uncomfortable? What sort of wonderful messages do we get from feeling bored, lonely or upset?'

There are some sad feelings that are completely appropriate. If someone we love dies, it is right that we feel grief. The feeling of sadness acknowledges their value to us and it helps us, one bit at a time, to accept our loss. Grief, sadness and anger and even boredom have value, but we don't need to be stuck in them. When we have accepted their meaning and their significance, we are free to move on.

People avoid uncomfortable emotions simply because they are uncomfortable, but if they just evade them, they lose out, because that discomfort has a purpose. It is a signal that it is time for something to change. That might be accepting a loss, or it might be that the judgement or belief in the emotion has to change. It might be that it is time for our behaviour to change. The five questions help us find out what has to change, and when the right change is made, the feeling changes too.

Changing emotions

Our emotions colour our entire experience. When we feel sad or lonely, the whole of us feels sad or lonely. It is not like having just another idea. It is more like a colour filter that affects everything we see. That often makes us feel and behave as though the emotion we feel right now is permanent, or it is the 'truth'. Well, it certainly is true, it is what you are feeling, but it is changeable. It may change at any moment. That fact is easily overlooked precisely because emotions are so all-encompassing. Furthermore, emotions are not rational and they are more powerful than reason. In stressful situations, such as a divorce, people may say and do all sorts of things that are not in their own or their children's best interests and they even may claim to be being rational. However, emotions can dominate our experience to such an extent that our mind thinks up reasons to justify what we feel.

When you feel good, the world looks like a good place. When you feel bad, the world looks bad. So it makes sense to maximize your ability to feel good. I have a high-achieving friend who gets positively excited when his business has a crisis. He enjoys the novelty, and the creativity required to find the solution.

Many feelings change spontaneously. They also change when we grasp the message they are sending us. So the key to changing any emotion is understanding the message. That means that we must turn towards it and feel it without rejecting it or judging it. Just feel it and then ask the Five Questions. Sometimes we have to ask the questions over and over again. Many times the feelings change as we ask questions. But wherever you start from, as you feel and experience your emotions you can explore the judgements inside them and find out if they are still true for you. If the judgements are not true, you can let them go and the feeling changes. If they are true, you can accept them; you change and your values change. Either way, you will feel better.

Avoidance

A great deal of human activity is geared towards distracting us from our emotions and covering them over with other feelings and activities. So much so that we have become used to doing it. But if we don't feel, we don't grow up. And the same emotions will keep coming up and asking for our attention until we notice them.

Again you may ask, if emotions have so much to offer, why is so much human activity geared towards avoiding them?

One of the big reasons on the outside is money. Apart from therapy, there is very little money in helping people to understand themselves. If people are unhappy and discontented, there is an awful lot of money to be made selling them things that will temporarily make them feel better. Food, fashion, shopping, drink and drugs all give people a temporary high. When it fades, as it does sooner or later, they can go back for more. That is repeat business. Economically that makes sense. People get pleasure from consumer goods and use the brands to create or bolster their identity.

The other big reason we avoid feelings is that so many of us have underrated ourselves. We fear that we won't be able to deal with what our emotions tell us. This fear is related to low self-esteem and a lack of love and trust in ourselves, which has been a human problem for ages, passed down from one generation to another. There is great opportunity in these times of relative wealth and peace to change those ancient, self-defeating patterns.

This system will help you feel good from the inside. What is more, as you process your own emotions, you will get to know yourself better and better and you won't need to use brands or possessions to build an image. You will discover your true self is more likeable and attractive than any image you tried to build in the past.

Tracking emotions

As we know, psychologists have demonstrated that what gets measured gets done. That applies to changing your emotional experience just as much as to moving to more satisfying and healthy eating. Therefore, I'd like you to write down whatever stands out most to you in your emotions each day. This is a very personal thing; there is no right or wrong. Just write down whatever you feel. As time passes you will begin to notice patterns and it may be helpful after a while to be able to look back and track your progress. But right now all you need to do is write down the most significant parts of your emotional experience. You can write a long essay if you want, but one or two sentences will do just as well.

EMOTIONAL SUCCESS TRACKER
Write down whatever part of your emotional experience stands out for you each day.

Do this every day for the next four weeks.

CHAPTER FIVE

•

An End to
Self-Sabotage

An end to self-sabotage

Self-sabotage is a mystery for so many people. Why do people stop themselves achieving what they want, particularly after making so much effort to get things right? How come they do it over and over again? What is happening? It is as though one part of them wants to succeed and another part wants to fail – hence the term 'self-sabotage'.

When we talk about parts here, we don't mean that we are actually divided into separate bits. It just refers to the fact that we can have two different desires which conflict. To make sense of the mystery, it is absolutely vital to grasp this fundamental truth about self-sabotage:

All dysfunctional behaviours have a positive intention.

The part that drives the sabotage behaviour is actually trying to help. I have discovered hundreds of different ways this occurs at my weight-loss seminars. For example, I worked with a woman who had dieted for months. One day when she was looking slim, a man chatted her up and instantly she felt compelled to eat. In the past when she was very slender she had had an affair. She loved her husband and the part that made her eat again was just trying to protect her marriage.

Another woman I met is a good example of this sort of behaviour. She told me that she had bought *I Can Make You Thin* but it hadn't worked for her. As you know, I always want to know why something doesn't work so that I can make it better. So I asked her what happened. It turned out that she hadn't listened to the CD. Not once. That explained why 'it hadn't worked'. She hadn't followed the instructions. But I wanted to know why. So I followed up and asked her why she hadn't ever listened to the Trance.

'Because you are going to make me hate chocolate,' she replied. That answer showed me she hadn't read the book properly either! However, I understood that there was a part of her that was trying to protect her. She got pleasure and comfort from eating chocolate and that part didn't want her to lose that pleasure and comfort. That part needed to know she could still eat chocolate and that she could get more pleasure and more comfort from other sources too.

Some people continually set goals, but never reach them because as soon as they notice they are succeeding, they feel a terrible compulsion to fail. They set about undermining their own achievements. I worked with a man who was almost successful over and over again, but at the last moment he would screw it up. Using hypnotic regression, we discovered that as a boy he had told his mother he wanted to be successful. She had said to him, 'Oh, you don't want to be successful. Successful people have heart attacks.' So on the very brink of success, his unconscious mind would make him fail because it was trying to protect him. With our conscious minds we know that rationally that is ridiculous. However, the unconscious is not logical. It is purposeful.

Other people have experienced failure in the past and it really hurt them. And the closer they got to their goals, the more painful the feeling of failure. Therefore, their unconscious mind tries to save them from suffering by getting the failure in quickly before it is too painful. Procrastinators are the same. They are not lazy, they are just frightened of failure because at some point in the past it hurt too much. They put off starting to avoid the pain of the failure they fear. In all of these cases the behaviour looks like self-sabotage, but behind it is the positive intention of self care.

Another type of self-sabotage happens when people who have been overweight for so long have an unconscious belief that 'the real me' is overweight. They don't like feeling fat, they might be very critical of themselves, but the hidden belief is created because unconsciously they have adapted to that body shape. So when they lose weight, a part of their mind feels they are abandoning who they really are, and it wants to eat to protect what it believes is their true self. Here again there is a negative outcome but a positive intention.

Some people have dinner with friends in a restaurant and stick religiously to a diet. They count calories or they eat lots of vegetables, they don't eat chips or bread or dessert. Then they go home and eat an entire packet of biscuits and a whole cake. That looks like self-sabotage. Why would anyone do it? They do it because the diet they are on has stressed them out and their method of stress control is eating. Remember the unconscious mind is purposeful but not logical. They are not thinking 'I must undermine myself' or 'I must have food'. One part of them is trying to lose weight, the other part is trying to control stress. This is like driving down the street with one foot on the accelerator and one on the brake. It just damages the car.

Stopping self-sabotage

Self-sabotage is just an unfortunate consequence of the way our brains work, but it is not inevitable, nor incurable. My friend Dr Richard Bandler has created a wonderful technique* that removes self-sabotage by integrating the differing parts or directions of our motivation.

I have put this technique on the CD and written it out below. Some people find they can read the instructions and then do the exercise easily. However, most people tell me they prefer to be guided through it. So please read the instructions now so that you know what to expect, and then relax and let me help you.

STOPPING SELF-SABOTAGE

You can use this exercise any time you feel an impulse to self-sabotage.

1. Identify a part of you that has an impulse to self-sabotage. If you have several, pick one for now.
2. Now ask your unconscious mind to identify a part of you that is the exact opposite, for example, a part that wants you to get to your ideal weight and be fully in touch with and in charge of your emotions.
3. Place your hands out in front of you, palms up. Imagine the part that wants to sabotage in your left hand, and the part that wants you to achieve your goal in your right hand.

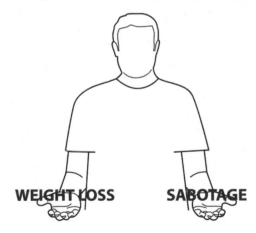

WEIGHT LOSS   SABOTAGE

4. Both parts have a positive intention for you, but they are going about it in different ways. You don't need to know what those intentions are, but keeping in mind that they

do have positive intentions, bring your hands very slowly together, no faster than feels comfortable. As you do this, it instructs your unconscious mind to create a union between the two parts, which finds a new way for them both to fulfil their positive intention. So, for example, it will create a way for you to become thinner and to feel safe.

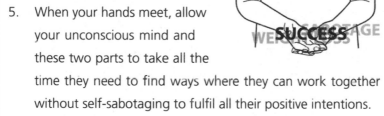

5.   When your hands meet, allow your unconscious mind and these two parts to take all the time they need to find ways where they can work together without self-sabotaging to fulfil all their positive intentions.

6.   When it feels complete – maybe it's like a click or a warm feeling or just a sense that they can work together – bring your hands into your chest and take the new integrated part inside you, and notice how good that feels.

7.   Now take a moment to imagine living your life with the benefit of this new integrated motivation. See yourself continuing all the way to success in weight loss and emotional freedom, and in all areas of your life.

There are also other triggers for self-sabotage and other ways to deal with them. In the section below I look at the basic psychology behind them, then I list the most common ones and simple ways to overcome them.

Automation

Many of us have accumulated habits which are accidentally counterproductive. Some love to come home and unwind in front of the TV with a beer or a glass of wine and a big bag of crisps. They aren't hungry, they don't actually need the alcohol, but they have associated the idea of TV, alcohol and crisps with relaxing. By the way, if you find yourself doing that sort of thing, the solution is simple. Before you switch on the TV, take twenty minutes to listen to the Trance. That way you give yourself proper, deep, healthy relaxation, and you can enjoy watching TV without needing beer and crisps.

Some people don't wait to get home to offload their stress. At my seminars I've met women from all over the world who have a chocolate drawer or a packet of cookies or a secret food stash at the office which they hit when they get stressed. They aren't trying to eat too much, they've just found a way to change how they feel.

Self-sabotage is not a deliberate intention to make a mess. It is just that different parts of us are trying to help in conflicting ways. It looks mysterious because we are not consciously choosing these behaviours. They have become automatic. The same habit-forming mechanism that makes our minds so quick and useful makes processes automatic even if we didn't choose them or we no longer want them. We will look at how these mechanisms can trip us up, and modify them to stop that happening.

Association

Perhaps the most basic function of the brain is association. We create associations all the time. In its simplest form, when we perceive two things together, the next time we perceive one it will remind us of the other. If there is a strong emotion evoked at the same time, the recall becomes more likely. The most famous example of this was the experiment carried out by Russian physiologist Ivan Pavlov. Whenever he fed his dogs, he would ring a bell. Very soon his dogs would salivate as soon as he rang the bell.

The more times we perceive the things together, the stronger the link between the two, and the more likely that each one perceived individually will cause us to think of the other.

Physiologically these links correspond to a string of neurons communicating with each other in your brain. The more often the link is perceived or remembered, the more often the neurons communicate, and the smoother and quicker the communication. A neural pathway is created and it is strengthened every time it is used.

Associations help us make sense of the world and navigate it safely. It is very helpful to associate the sight of flames with heat and to associate the sound of a horn with warning. But the process of making associations is indiscriminate. The mind doesn't make only helpful associations. It just keeps making them, all day, every day, regardless of whether they are helpful or useful.

Momentum

Our minds have momentum. When we are awake, we are thinking almost all the time, and one thought leads to another and another and another, all day long. It is very rare, and mostly takes a great deal of training, to experience a mind that is awake and aware but not thinking.

Momentum and associations combine to create the simplest and most common form of self-sabotage. In the days when you used to do emotional eating, it became associated at random with all sorts of other things in your life. It could be a piece of music, a café you passed, a boss who annoyed you, thinking of a friend or remembering a holiday. Emotional eating was arbitrarily associated with any number of things. If you came across those things in your everyday life, or even if they just came to mind, they could evoke memories of, and cravings for, emotional eating. Your life was littered with random associations to emotional eating that could be triggered at any point. Many of these associations have nothing to do with eating, or food, or feelings or weight, they are only part of your old way of life, which included emotional eating.

As you stop emotional eating, all the patterns associated with it have to change too. There are so many potential associations to emotional eating that it is impossible to predict where, when or how they might be triggered. It sounds like a nightmare – and before you started using this, perhaps it was.

The solution, however, is simple. We can't fight the process of association, nor the momentum of the mind. We will use them. We will use the same forces that create the problem to create the solution. We will create a new neural pathway so that the impulse to do emotional eating leads to a more rewarding outcome.

Imagination

Look around you now. Everything manufactured, from a teaspoon to a skyscraper, was once just an idea in someone's head. Unless you are out in the wilderness, even the land around you was shaped by a human intervention that was first merely an idea. Everything we have created, we first imagined.

However, imagination does not create only machines and buildings and works of art. The imagination is easily activated by everyday habits and associations. One of the old habits was emotional eating. You may remember that when you used to do emotional eating you could find yourself imagining eating long before you did it.

You may have thought that didn't matter because there are no calories in an idea. However, we know that at a certain neurological level, the mind does not distinguish between a real event and a vividly imagined one. Imagining the act of eating reinforces the pattern in the same way as actually doing it. We need to guide your imagination to reinforce your new patterns of healthier eating.

We can't stop the imagination working, any more than we can stop the mind thinking. The solution is to redirect it. So instead of imagining eating, we learn to imagine something a great deal better.

How to stop 'sabotage thinking'

Automation, association, momentum and imagination all combine to create what I call 'sabotage thinking'. Old emotional patterns influence the rational part of the mind, so people find themselves making up reasons for abandoning their decision to change for the better. These ideas are the exact opposite of what they really want. This type of thinking is very common, very tiring and completely unhelpful. I have written out the most common varieties below. See if any of them apply to you. If they do, use the solution beneath to get rid of them.

Sabotage Thinking 1
Casual association

This happens when the mind wanders around close to old patterns as though it didn't matter because we don't feel like eating. For example, we walk past a patisserie and look at a lemon meringue pie. We don't normally eat that sort of thing so it seems innocent enough. 'I wonder what that tastes like,' we think, and out of mere curiosity we walk in and find out how much it costs. 'Oh, that's not so much,' we think, and the saleswoman is very welcoming ... and suddenly we are on the brink of eating something we don't want and don't need because of entertaining casual thoughts.

> ## SOLUTION
> **Stick to the Four Golden Rules!**
>
> **Remember, genuine hunger is not
> triggered by association.
> It comes on slowly and persists.**

Sabotage Thinking 2
I'm doing so well I deserve a treat

There are many different variations on this theme. Many people are amazed at how quickly they change and they get quite a high from their rapid success. When you have faced old demons and discovered that they are no longer as scary as they once were, you feel pretty good. And when you have eaten healthily for just a few days, your body feels better already. That's when this thinking kicks in. 'Look, I've done so well,' the mind says, 'let's celebrate – by eating!'

Or maybe you feel a bit tired. 'I've done the work,' says the mind, 'now I deserve a treat. Let's have a little feast just like the old days!'

Another version goes something like this: 'I've completed a whole month of my new way of life. I feel great, I weigh less, I understand myself and my feelings a whole lot more. I deserve something to celebrate this milestone. Why don't I just eat a lot?'

SOLUTION
You just need to see that this idea of celebration or reward is based on the past when food was a guilty pleasure.
Now you are already enjoying food every single day.
You need to find a bigger, better way to celebrate!

Sabotage Thinking 3
A tiny bit won't hurt

Sometimes old habits crop up and your mind thinks, 'Hey, a tiny bit won't hurt.' For example, if you used to eat a whole packet of biscuits in the days of emotional eating, you might find yourself looking at a packet in a supermarket and thinking, 'Hey, one biscuit won't hurt.' Rationally, you are right. But this is not a rational situation. You can tell that the mind is making up a justification to carry on the old emotional eating habit because the first thought is not, 'I am hungry.' If you are not hungry, there is no need to eat. It is not the biscuit that would hurt, but the feeding of the old habit.

It is also interesting because it is a sort of double negative – it won't hurt. But what will it do that is a benefit? Always look carefully at these double negatives and seek out the positive desire. You want to eat a biscuit? That is not much of a benefit. Is that actually what you want? Maybe you want to feel better. Maybe you really want a hug or a cuddle.

SOLUTION
Whenever you find your mind thinking, 'Such and such won't hurt,' ask two questions:
1. If I express it in positive terms, what will it do?
2. What do I really want?

Sabotage Thinking 4
This doesn't really count ...

When you have established your new patterns, the old ones take some time to fade away. The mind has a tendency to want to cling to the old habits, but it is blocked by your new behaviours. So it tries to get them back in a roundabout way. For example, imagine that your old emotional eating habit revolved around chocolate: chocolate bars, chocolate cakes, chocolate drinks. You have now moved on and you feel great. Everything is going brilliantly. One day you find yourself day-dreaming about desserts. You don't normally eat dessert, but after lunch you order a dessert. You eat a few mouthfuls, you feel full and you've had enough – but you find yourself thinking, 'Well, it's not chocolate, so this doesn't really count.'

This is an argument from the bad old days of dieting. Something does or doesn't 'count' if you are following some arbitrary regime or counting calories. You are not doing that any more. The real questions to ask are, 'Am I hungry?' and 'Is this mouthful completely enjoyable?'

SOLUTION

Don't get caught up in wondering whether or not something 'counts'. Just follow the Four Golden Rules. That's it. Debating irrelevant points is confusing and irritating. Stick to the rules.

Sabotage Thinking 5
It's not me, it's just an instinct

This is the belief that because a desire arises by itself, the outcome is uncontrollable. In fact, all sorts of thoughts arise unbidden in our minds and they just drift away or get forgotten. The mind here is latching on to this perfectly normal process and trying to use it as an excuse to behave in the same way. But just because a thought arises by itself, it doesn't mean we are compelled to act on it. We are not in charge of spontaneous thoughts, we are in charge of our responses.

SOLUTION
Stick to the Four Golden Rules! Remember,
genuine hunger is not triggered by association.
It comes on slowly and persists.

Sabotage Thinking 6
I just want to feel something familiar

You are changing a lot. Emotional eating had a huge effect on your life. Stepping free of it is like a new start in life. You now have new ways to relax, new ways to work and new ways to feel good. There is so much that's new that at some point you may want to feel something familiar. Emotional eating was a familiar form of comfort.

SOLUTION
It is comforting to have some familiar experience when there is so much change. Don't fight this desire, but find a different comforting, familiar experience. It might be curling up on the sofa with a good book or your favourite DVD. It might be calling up an old friend. It might be something even simpler, like taking extra care in the morning to put on your favourite clothes.

Sabotage Thinking 7
The Vortex

There are times when an idea just gets stuck in your head. You can't stop thinking about it. If that thought is about eating, it can be infuriating. The way I think about this is not so much that an idea is stuck in your head, but rather that your head is stuck in an idea. Whichever way you turn, that idea keeps popping up. You try to ignore it, and two minutes later it comes right back at you.

SOLUTION: ESCAPE THE VORTEX

This is an example of the imagination being more powerful than the will, so we'll use the imagination to deal with it. Any idea is made of pictures or words, or both, in our minds.

1. If the idea has a picture, notice where you see it – to your left, or right, above, level with or below your eyeline.

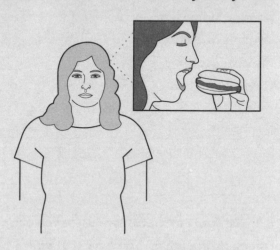

2. Wherever It Is, shrink it, drain out the colour so it is black and white and move it off into the dIstance.

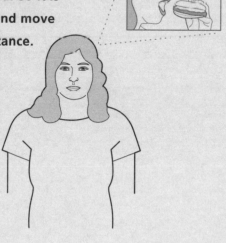

3. Finally reduce it to the size of a postage stamp and send it away into the distance, way, way behind you.

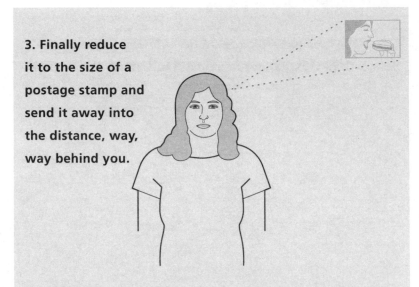

4. If the idea has words, we use a voice in our head to hear them. Notice where you hear that voice, then move it out so it seems to be coming from the tip of your thumb.

5. Now change the voice to something ridiculous, like Donald Duck.

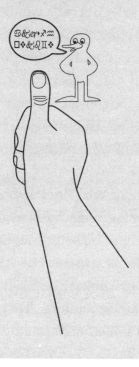

The Monkey Mind

Thousands of years ago, the Buddha likened human consciousness to a gang of crazy monkeys all clamouring for attention. He called it the Monkey Mind. All self-sabotage and mental confusion are manifestations of this monkey mind. Mental momentum and association combine with random arguments to form the continual stream of one thought after another after another. This mental chatter is like a radio station you can't turn off, and it is completely independent of your true desires.

I have a neighbour who does a short yoga routine every morning. One morning I congratulated him on his discipline. 'Oh no,' he said, 'I have no self-discipline at all. That's why I have this routine. If I had to think about it every day I'd give up in no time. But I've made a habit so I unroll my yoga mat before I've really started thinking. That gets me going.'

Then he added something I found even more interesting. The terrace where he does his yoga is a few metres from his bedroom. He told me that very often when he is walking from his bedroom to the terrace he thinks, 'I can't be bothered to do yoga this morning, I'll give it a miss today.' Then his mind rushes ahead to the pleasure of eating breakfast and all the more important things he has to do during the day.

In reality, from the perspective of a happy, healthy and fulfilled life, there is nothing more important for him than those ten minutes of stretching in the morning. They keep his body fit, they set him up for the day, he likes the sense of achievement, and after the first stretch he enjoys the physical feeling as his body wakes up and stretches out. What's not to like? But *still* that 'I can't be bothered' thought goes through his head, even though he has continually and consistently disagreed with it for years. So he has learned to just keep going, get to his mat and start his yoga.

That inner conversation beautifully illustrates the monkey mind. He knows what he wants and he does it. But even so the monkey mind makes up thoughts that are completely opposed to what he really wants because the monkey mind loves to make up excuses for us to do nothing and to sit around and fantasize even when we actually do want to make an effort.

We are all capable of taming the monkey mind. The Buddha taught meditation to help his students calm down their minds. If you practise meditation, you'll find it helps too. But if you don't have time for that, use the solutions in this chapter to get help straight away. Each time you use a solution, you reinforce the new pattern it creates, taking you away from self-sabotage and towards the solution. This is the education your mind needs, practising procedures to tame the monkeys and bring you to inner content and outer success. The antidote to the monkey mind is two-fold: practise positive habits, and keep connected to your deepest desires.

You don't have to wait for all the monkeys to start clamouring to start improving things. You have a choice at the beginning of every day. You can start the day by focusing your mind on what is healthy and helpful. That is a great basis on which to plan the day's progress towards your success and happiness.

A GOOD START TO THE DAY

Write one positive goal for tomorrow, no matter big or small, at the top of tomorrow's page in your Success Tracker.

Do it now.

CHAPTER SIX

•

Handling Success

Handling success

If you look back over the big changes in your life, you will notice there are always two aspects: what changed within you and what changed around you. You are changing now on the inside. You are developing a more fulfilling relationship with yourself by processing your emotions and benefiting from the wisdom and sensitivity they bring. This is a very personal journey. As you let go of emotional eating, you become more and more open to the present.

Another entire area of your life will also change, which is your relationships with the people around you: family, friends, work colleagues, neighbours and acquaintances. You will become more confident and at ease in yourself.

All of this sounds wonderful, and it is. Is there a catch? No – but there is a challenge. When you change yourself, you change the dynamics of all your everyday relationships. You will need to adjust those relationships to enhance all that is good in them and leave behind the parts that were associated with emotional eating.

Systemic change

I worked with a woman who used to meet her best friend two or three times a week in a particular coffee shop. They both drank coffee and they both ate a cake. Sometimes they even bought another cake and shared it. They enjoyed the fact that whatever else was going on in their lives, they could enjoy a good chat together, and console each other if they had had a bad day. When my client stopped emotional eating, she discovered that she didn't want to eat every time she went to the coffee shop. She noticed she was often leaving most of her cake on her plate. She didn't even always have a coffee. Sometimes she ordered a chai or a herbal tea.

As time passed, she noticed two more things: first, it was harder to find the time to meet her best friend because her life had become so busy, and secondly, when they did meet, she wanted to talk about all the great stuff that was happening, and her friend seemed to have an awful lot of stories of disappointment. Meeting up wasn't so much fun any more. Subconsciously she started to find other things to do, and that made it worse because, when they did meet, her friend made comments about how she seemed to be avoiding her. Her new way of life was upsetting her old relationships.

It is helpful to realize that all the relationships between ourselves and others form a system. That system will have a natural tendency to seek a balance, and once it has found a balance, it will try to maintain it. When you change, you disrupt that balance. The system will seek to balance itself again, and there are two options. The first is to push you back into your old behaviours so the old patterns are re-stabilized. The second is to find a new arrangement that also creates balance.

From my client's point of view, she had two choices. On the one hand, she could go back to eating more cake than she needed and swapping stories of disappointment with her friend. That would be the old system balanced again. Alternatively, she could come to a new arrangement, such as meeting to do one of her new activities, like going for a walk or to a yoga class. If her friend agreed and they set up a new routine, that would create a new balance in their system.

Changing relationships

Change can be uncomfortable. Therefore, people may resist it instinctively without thinking, even if the end result will be good. Occasionally you will find that people around you react badly to your changes. You may find yourself involved in conflicts that upset your equilibrium and trigger a desire for the old habit of emotional eating.

In fact, any conflict or upsets can challenge your newly acquired habits or your equilibrium. So the best way to look after yourself includes looking after your relationships, to ensure all of them are as productive as possible.

I have a friend who has helped many women to lose weight over the years. He has guided them through the system in *I Can Make You Thin* and helped his clients with all the emotional and relationship issues that come up. He has a simple way of describing the problem. He says, 'Next to every woman struggling on a diet is a fat friend saying, "Never mind that, have another piece of cake."' As you lose weight and eat less, you may well leave behind some of the people with whom you shared bad eating habits.

As your relationships with people around you change, many different issues are affected. Some of them may not have anything to do with food. For example, you might find that you enjoy walking or cycling more, so you use your car less and you are no longer available to give a lift to a friend. The law of averages suggests that, as you change, some issues like this will come up and challenge you.

Your success in losing weight and in achieving greater emotional fulfilment may cause some of your old friends to be a bit resentful. People who've used my system have told me that their old friends who are on diets can't believe that they are losing weight and eating what they want. To put it bluntly, they are envious.

As you gain more control of your weight and your life, you get more power. With power comes responsibility. If your old friends are a bit resentful, it is down to you to make the best of the situation.

One of my friends who used this system ordered French fries when she had lunch with her old friends. She ate what she wanted and then stopped. There was about three-quarters of a bowl of French fries sitting on the table, taunting her friends who were on low-carb diets. That was funny, but it would be unkind to do it all the time. And some people have told me that some of their old friends have become quite unpleasant or sarcastic. Others have had trouble keeping the peace in families that have a history of overeating.

In all of these cases it is important to know how to get the best out of the situation, and to keep all the good parts of your family relationships and friendships.

Non-violent communication

As many of your relationships are going to be changing, I'd like to tell you about the work of an American psychologist called Marshall Rosenberg, which I have found inspiring because it is so simple and so useful. He has created an amazingly powerful approach to resolving situations that could lead to conflicts. Marshall saw a lot of violence in the neighbourhood in which he grew up. In 1943 he and his family spent three days locked inside their house as race riots raged around them. Outside, dozens of people were killed. At school he was attacked simply because of his ethnicity. These early incidents led him to a lifelong interest in promoting non-violence.

Marshall modestly says that he has made nothing new, but he has designed a way of talking that reduces the conflict in any communication between human beings. He calls it non-violent communication.*

Marshall believes that human behaviour is driven by our needs. We all need food, warmth and shelter. But beyond that, to live a rich and full human life we have many other needs. We need love and intimacy and beauty and self-respect and acceptance and stimulation and challenges and many other things.

He believes that each of us has the responsibility to

* To find out more about Marshall's work on Non-Violent Communication, see www.cnvc.org.

find strategies to meet our own needs. Sometimes we ask other people to meet our needs. Sometimes they agree, and sometimes they don't. If we state our feelings and our needs clearly, without any agenda of judgement or criticism, we are more likely to be helped. Furthermore, even if the person we ask doesn't want to meet our needs, when our communication is clear it is easier to move on without blame or criticism and find another person or strategy to meet those needs. Marshall's non-violent communication lets each of us state our needs and feelings clearly, and hear other people's needs and feelings clearly.

In Chapter Four you learned a better way to explore your own feelings for yourself. With Marshall's work we can use some of the information that process gives us to improve our relationships with others. The Five Questions help you understand your own situation better, and you can use that alongside non-violent communication to maximize the positives in your relationship with others.

Of course, many people speak with a lot of judgement and criticism and praise and blame, because that sort of language is all around us. So Marshall also shows how to listen with non-judgemental empathy. That means we don't hear criticisms or insults or judgements, we just listen out for the needs and feelings behind people's words. When we listen to those and respond to those, people feel truly heard and we can bypass any conversations about criticisms. At his workshops, Marshall works with couples, and by using this sort of language he has shown them how to resolve arguments and disagreements that have sometimes lasted for decades. These simple changes in language can have a miraculous effect.

Dissolving conflict

The best way to avoid conflict is to recognize our own needs and those of others, but to keep judgement and criticism out of our communication. This is a little more difficult than it sounds because there is so much judgement built into our everyday speech that often we don't notice it. However, with a bit of practice we soon get better at it.

Marshall suggests that we think of our communication in four parts, and keep each part simple and separate.

1. Say what you observe

First, say what you observe as objectively as possible. Avoid being critical or judgemental. This sounds simple but it takes practice because many common words have criticism built into them. For example, 'When I hear you speaking' is neutral. It is not judgemental. However, 'When you criticize me' is itself a critical way of describing the speech. The trick is to find a neutral, objective description of things.

If we go back to the example above, my client could say, 'I notice that I am less interested in eating cake and drinking coffee these days.' That is an honest, objective description, and there is no criticism of herself or her friend in it.

2. Say what you feel

Secondly, state how you feel. Importantly, we each need to take responsibility for our own emotions. For example, when I say, 'I feel fearful', I am taking responsibility for my own emotions. If I said, 'You make me scared', I would imply you are responsible for my emotions. That would not be helpful because it could be heard as blaming you. Ultimately no one can make you feel anything. Feelings arise as you perceive events, and you have a choice about how you respond to them.

In our example my client could say, 'And I feel frustrated.'

3. State your needs

Your feelings arise because of the interaction between what you experience and what you need. Every feeling has an underlying need. If the need is met, I feel good; if the need is not met, the feeling is prompting me to create a strategy to get that need met.

Carrying on with our example, my client could add, 'Because I have needs for both affection and stimulation.'

4. Make your request

If you have a request of someone else, make it of a specific action. That helps them know what to do to meet your need. A request such as, 'I want you to love me more' is doubly impossible to grant. First, because it asks someone to feel something. Feelings arise spontaneously from our needs and situations. We can't just make them up. Secondly, this request doesn't say what they are being asked to do. 'Please take some time to give me a hug' is a specific, doable, observable action. It is a functional request.

Claims, demands and orders can create conflict or repression. Always phrase your wishes as requests and always recognize that people are free to agree or to decline them. If someone agrees freely to my request, then there will be no resentment.

To finish off our example with my client, she could continue, 'So I would like to meet those needs with you by meeting at a place where we can do something active together.'

If my coffee shop client used these exact words she might sound a bit clunky, but she is saying what she observes, feels, needs and wants, all without any criticism of herself or her friend. That makes it easier for her friend to reply honestly and express her feelings and needs. She is free to agree or make an alternative suggestion. I'm illustrating this with a very small, everyday example to show how this model can be applied anywhere there is a potential conflict.

Practice

I would like you to practise using these four steps at least once a day. Even if you don't have anything to discuss, arrange or sort out with anyone, you can notice your own feelings and go through the process yourself. Alternatively, you can practise with a friend. If something bothers you, try to say what you observe, and ask your friend to help you check that there is only objective observation and no criticism in your words.

Going carefully through these four steps can feel a bit awkward at first, but in the end that is better than having an argument, especially as it makes reaching a resolution much, much easier. And the more you practise, the easier it gets.

The key is to state, without criticism or judgement:

1. **What you observe.**
2. **What you feel.**
3. **What your need is.**
4. **What you request.**

Remember, you may not get number 4 from the person you are talking to, but this is your best chance of doing so. If you don't get it, this is your best chance of moving on amicably.

Listening empathically

Of course, the person we are talking to may have no interest in non-violent communication. That doesn't matter. We can apply the same principles to listening as to speaking. Marshall suggests that when we listen to people, we don't pay attention to judgements or criticisms, but we do pay attention to the feelings and needs behind their words.

That is easy to write, but it takes a while to get the hang of it. We are programmed by our competitive society to be defensive or aggressive when we hear anything that sounds like criticism. You will find that the confidence, calm and equanimity you have gained from the process you learned in Chapter Four will be an enormous help.

Your daily practice will help, too, so when you make and hear requests, you naturally focus on what you observe and feel, and you recognize your own needs and those of others. It will soon become second nature to communicate like this. You won't do it perfectly all the time, and that is absolutely fine.

Relationships

Non-violent communication can have an almost miraculous effect on relationships, but I don't want you to get the idea that these four steps will make everything all right ever after. Something you'll notice quite soon is that your relationships cause emotions to arise within you which, on examination, may have little to do with the people you are talking to. They may be just your own business, so you need to process them using the Five Questions we looked at in Chapter Four.

Relationships are a part of our life in which we can learn a great deal, because the people we get close to get close enough to touch our sore spots. You may find you clarify a disagreement with a partner, but then have to work through some of your own feelings before you can work with them or get close to them again. The good thing is that using the Five Questions and non-violent communication, you can work things through. No matter how complicated or difficult things appear, these two techniques will get you through, one step at a time. On the way you will learn more about yourself and your partner, and you will increase both your compassion and your resilience.

CHAPTER SEVEN

•

Your New Life

Your new life

Millions of people have used my system to lose weight. At my seminars I have personally met thousands of people who are losing weight and for the first time in their lives feel happy in their bodies. However, a good number have told me they are angry at all the time and money they wasted on diet clubs. They also resent the fact that they were led to believe losing weight was going to be a struggle. When you embrace and process your emotions, you do use and release energy and it can be exciting, but it is not a hard slog. It is really an adventure.

When I see fat on a person's body, I see layers and layers of frustration and anger and years of dieting and getting bigger and bigger. I passionately believe we can leave all that behind. Diets have had their day. In the richest nations in the world, where there is more food than we could possibly eat or need, people are starving themselves to get thin. It would be hilarious if it wasn't so sad.

The irony is that the diets that claim to reduce obesity make things worse. Seventy per cent of dieters end up heavier than before. The more diets they do, the heavier they get. I get angry because these statistics are in the public domain. I believe the diet clubs and food-substitute salesmen often know their products don't work, but still take your money.

Sometimes people tell me that they dieted and they nearly succeeded. They tell me it worked for three months until it all went wrong. I don't actually believe it worked at all, ever.

During those three months that person was continually on the case, counting calories, avoiding carbs or whatever the diet demanded, but essentially they were starving themselves. They were tricked into thinking they had success, but it was a sham. The moment they stopped dieting, their poor starved body went into overdrive to fight back against the months of deprivation.

Dieting doesn't establish a safe, stable, healthy body, it just slows the metabolism and puts the body into starvation mode. That is not a success.

Right now, you are part of the change that makes a genuine difference. You are not fighting your body, you are working with it. The world at large is full of people who simply follow trends and allow themselves to be victims of corporations selling food they don't need and diet clubs selling solutions that don't work. You have chosen to tread a different path, one of personal responsibility for your own weight and emotional health. I offer you my congratulations and I have the utmost respect for your willingness to put the time and energy into this path.

You can read this book from cover to cover in less than one day, but the changes you start today will affect the rest of your life. For one week you will watch the DVD, listen to the Trance and use the 'Listen While You Eat' recording at least once a day. You will write down what you ate and what you felt each day in your Success Tracker. Within this week you will experience extraordinary changes. As you carry on you will become a new version of yourself: happier, slimmer, healthier and more confident.

When you lose weight, you will also shed the emotional baggage of feelings that were repressed as those extra pounds piled on, so from time to time you'll experience emotions that seem to have little if anything to do with what is going on right now. These are emotions that have been frozen in the past. You are now able to process your emotions properly, so your unconscious mind knows that you are able to deal with them. You can use Havening to manage their intensity and the Five Questions to unfold them.

Release

I have never had issues with my weight, but I come from an overweight family, and, like every other person on this planet, I have had to learn how to accept and appreciate the intelligence of my own emotions.

Not so long ago I got very down. I had been working very hard, a relationship had finished and I had suffered a number of bereavements. I was working with people who were very depressed. In the end, I became very down myself. I got a phone call from a friend of mine, Genpo Roshi, who is a Zen master.

He said, 'I hear you've been down. Why didn't you call me?'

And I said, 'Because there is no point in anything.'

The world looked grey and empty to me, as it does to everyone who is depressed.

Then he said to me out of the blue, 'I want to talk to the voice of depression disowned.' He didn't say 'the voice of depression' but 'depression *disowned*'.

I was surprised. I had no idea that I had disowned depression in the past. Anyway, I turned my attention inwards and asked myself if there was a part of me that was depression disowned. To my surprise I found myself saying, 'Yes, there is an aspect of me that is depressed and disowned.'

He said, 'Why were you disowned?'

I replied, 'Because it was too uncomfortable to cope with it. I couldn't bear it.'

Genpo asked, 'How does it feel to be disowned?'

I said, 'Depressing! And upsetting. In fact, I decided that I never wanted to experience it again.'

Because I'd kept this aspect of me disowned, it had always been looking for a way to express itself. It was waiting for a time when I wasn't busy, working or actively making myself happy so that it could emerge and deliver its message. I had assumed that I should be happy all the time. That created stress by denying my true feelings.

Genpo showed me a wonderful way to work with disowned emotions so that we can integrate them and their wisdom into our lives.

When I accepted the feelings of sadness were real and belonged to me, I felt them. I felt the grief at my loss and then the grief came to an end. It was gone, and I felt a blissful calmness and appreciation of the present moment. I had had no idea how much awareness I had been missing. By denying that sadness, I had undervalued myself and blocked a part of my emotional sensitivity. As I accepted it and let it pass through me, I also freed up that section of my emotional sensitivity so I could feel my experience more richly and more deeply.

Genpo believes that we disown, marginalize or squash down those parts of us that are too uncomfortable for us to handle. He has created a beautiful and simple technique to release those emotions safely and carefully.

Disowned emotions

I have since used Genpo's technique with many people. For example, I worked with a young girl once who had a rage disorder. Her father had quite a temper. She had learned from him how easy it was to get angry. However, if she ever got angry, she was berated and told she was a bad girl and she was in trouble. As a result, she had squashed her anger down for so long that it had started to come out in a totally uncontrolled way. If someone stood on her foot by accident, she would hit them. It had reached the point where she had hit so many people that if she hit one more she was going to prison.

I started by asking if I could speak to rage disowned. Although she was quite a petite girl, she suddenly became really scary.

She hissed, 'You are speaking to rage disowned.'

'How does it feel to be disowned?' I asked.

'It makes me furious!'

'Why were you disowned?'

'Because people said it wasn't right for a girl to get so mad and it wasn't right for me to lose my temper, and that made me even more angry! Eventually I couldn't stand it any more and I lashed out.'

Once I had let rage disowned have its say, she felt much calmer. I knew, however, that the ability to be angry is important for all of us. She needed to be able to get angry in a healthy way, just as we all do. So I helped her to incorporate it using Genpo Roshi's approach.

I asked her to remember the rage again but also at the same time to remember what it is like to feel peace, the complete opposite of her rage. This is how we did it. I would like to share this process with you now.

Most of us, like me, don't realize that we have disowned emotions. We feel low or depressed but we honestly don't know why. If you feel like that, or if you feel that you absolutely don't know why you find yourself doing emotional eating, the following exercise is perfect for you.

I have written it out here, but if you prefer to listen to it and do it with me as I talk to you, you can use the CD. Read it through first, however, so you know what to expect.

EMOTIONAL BALANCING

This exercise helps you integrate the experience and wisdom of feelings that have been suppressed. You can use it as often as necessary to bring balance to every level of your emotions.

1. Close your eyes and place your hands in front of you, slightly apart, palms up.
2. Invite your unconscious mind to identify an emotion that is disowned, and imagine placing it on your left hand. If you find that difficult, imagine holding a little parcel in that hand which contains the emotion within it.
3. Invite the disowned emotion to communicate to you what it wants to say that you haven't heard.
4. Just listen to whatever comes up.
5. When it has finished communicating, invite your unconscious mind to find the opposite of this emotion (for example, if it's anger, find peace).
6. Imagine that feeling sitting in your right hand. Let yourself experience it as strongly as you can.
7. Now, move your attention to just above your head and keep it there.
8. With your attention above your head, experience the two emotions at the same time. Keep your attention just above your head so it feels as if you are looking down on both feelings and experiencing them simultaneously.

9. Stay like this for as long as you need, until you can feel a stable and secure sense of balance, and you know that it's possible to experience both of these emotions and that they have recalibrated the way they signal to you. Now that the emotion is not disowned, it will not need to signal so strongly in future, unless it's an exceptional situation. So you will find you have more emotional equilibrium.

10. When the balance is established, relax and drop your hands. This process allows the emotions to recalibrate and coexist peacefully. Each one is then available, when necessary, to guide you and inform you.

Techniques of personal change

During the first week, give your full attention to all the exercises, the recordings and the DVD, exactly as I have asked. After that, I have suggested a minimum programme of using the Trance each week and regular use of the 'Listen While You Eat' recording and the sessions of Havening, with or without the DVD. Genpo's Emotional Balancing exercise is a beautiful and gentle way to integrate disowned emotions. Use it, and the other exercises, as and when you need them. Do what works for you.

The whole process recalibrates your emotions and puts you in charge of your response to them. That sets you free to enjoy your food, and you never need to use it to squash your emotions.

This process is both dramatic and gradual. There is a wonderful feeling of elation as you start to change, and you feel the uplift from the Havening work immediately. The everyday habits of eating change quickly as you follow the Four Golden Rules. Other things change more gradually. The weight loss is gradual. Relationships and other parts of your life develop day by day as you achieve more emotional sensitivity and freedom.

Your new sensitivity may lead you to make changes you did not expect. You may notice that your habits of speech change. Instead of putting a brave face on about feeling overweight, you will feel genuinely good, and that will be reflected in more optimistic language. When you go out to eat with friends, you don't have to push your food around your plate and secretly plan to go home and binge. You can eat what you like, enjoy it and, when you are full, stop.

You will find you relate differently to family and friends and even to strangers. You are more confident and at ease in yourself; you will find it easier to be friendly and strike up conversations. You will also find it easier to maintain your boundaries, protect your own interests and ensure you have appropriate privacy and safety.

Serious

There will be moments when you suddenly realize that this is serious. Not because food or even weight loss is that important, but because your life is important. It is the only one you have and you are the only person who can live it.

As you regain your full emotional range and establish a deeper sense of balance and self-worth, you really can feel that every day is a wonder, a miracle to be enjoyed to the full. That doesn't mean doing things to excess. It does mean giving your full attention to whatever you are doing so that you relish every part of your life. Of course, we all get tired; we can't live in a state of total alertness all the time. But we can make the most of our lives by making the most of what is right in front of us right now. The more you connect to life emotionally, the more it rewards you.

Evidence

Use the Success Tracker at the back of this book to keep track of your progress. Don't take progress for granted or mistake it for wishful thinking. Write down how you eat and what you feel. You will know real change is taking place when you are absolutely sure that three things are happening:

1. **You eat differently. You compare what you ate and how you ate with what you are eating now, and it has changed.**
2. **Your body is different. You have moved towards your ideal weight and you feel more comfortable in your own skin.**
3. **You feel better emotionally. You feel stronger and calmer, capable of experiencing sad, painful or challenging feelings without having to distract yourself, and capable of enjoying good feelings completely, with a real sense of entitlement to joy.**

When you use this system and follow the instructions, all three things will happen. Each one may take a different time to become manifest for different people, but all of them will happen for you.

As time passes you will notice that you are less and less interested in writing about food, because you simply won't be thinking about it so much. By tuning in to your body's wisdom, you will eat when you are hungry, enjoy every mouthful and stop as soon as you feel full. Simple and delicious.

On the other hand, your feelings will become more and more interesting. As you engage more and more at the emotional level, your life and the discoveries it offers become more and more rewarding. Each of us is unique, so I have no idea what your personal journey of fulfilment will be, but I do know it will be challenging from time to time, and also offer a deep and richer satisfaction with life.

Normal

Occasionally people tell me they just want to be 'normal'. Nowadays I'm not convinced 'normal' is such a great idea. In the developed world, millions and millions of people are overweight. In the UK a quarter and in the USA more than a third of all adults are clinically obese. So being overweight is accepted as pretty normal. Emotional eating seems normal too.

A lot of what people do is activity to keep their minds occupied without too much room for feeling. More and more people suffer from addictions: drink, drugs, online gaming, pornography, work, exercise and many others. More widespread than any of these obvious addictions, however, is overeating. Food has become the Western world's drug of choice. Bingeing, night-time eating, grazing, snacking and gorging are commonplace. Obesity is now the biggest and most costly cause of physical and mental ill-health in the West.

From this point of view we could say that what is 'normal' now is not healthy. I would rather you go for being just a bit better off than normal.

That means you don't just follow the herd. You are in charge of your own life, your own activities. Now that you are changing how you feel, it is a good time to change other parts of your life. It is time to explore new routes to personal fulfilment.

Physical activity

Your new way of life is going to include more physical activity. Just as your body knows what to eat, it also knows what to do to keep healthy. You will find you begin to seek out new ways to be active. Being active is not an ordeal. Your body will actually prompt you to do it because it is a natural part of the healthy life of your body.

For some of you this will be quite a surprise. When your body is heavy, even ordinary activity can be exhausting. But as you get lighter and lighter, your muscles will be looking for ways to be used and keep toned. A few of you may choose to go to the gym, but many of you will find yourselves choosing less obvious ways to enjoy your fitness. It may be hill-walking or ballroom dancing. It could be Sunday afternoon football. I don't know what it is, and maybe you don't know what it is either. If you don't have any idea yet, just watch out for that feeling of physical restlessness and then experiment. Go for an introductory class in something, and see how you feel. This is not necessarily something you can work out in advance with your head. Just try anything and see how you actually feel when you've tried it.

Change is not a privilege

Diet clubs make weight loss seem expensive and difficult. Psychoanalysts make personal change look like a long and expensive exploration of the deepest, darkest secrets. Academic psychologists can make emotional intelligence look difficult. But it's not!

Weight loss should not be a big business sector which exploits the same people over and over again as they join diet clubs, lose muscle mass, starve themselves and then pile the weight back on again. Personal change does not have to take years of therapy, or cost a fortune. Emotional intelligence is not a magic privilege for a few lucky, rich people; it is a natural capacity we all reach through processing exactly what we feel and learning from our experience.

We can all make amazing positive changes by taking small, simple steps each day. I have worked with people from all walks of life with all sorts of problems stemming from a huge range of causes. Some have experienced the horrors of war and abuse too terrible to write about. Others come from backgrounds that appear to have all the privileges that wealth can afford and yet on the inside are a living hell.

All these people came to me because they had symptoms they believed they could never overcome on their own, and one of the most common of those symptoms was weight issues. All of them found that the solution was much, much simpler than they imagined. I showed them the very same techniques and exercises that I have now shown you. And they changed. They lost weight and now enjoy life more than ever before.

The future

I see excess weight as the physical manifestation of past sorrow. As you lose weight, you no longer have to carry that sorrow around with you. Sometimes you have to feel it before it goes, sometimes it just melts away.

The better you feel and the fitter you get, the more confident you are and the less fear you have of the future. So as you move away from past sorrow and worries about the future, you are genuinely free to enjoy the present more and more. That is the real freedom that this book is bringing to you. To prepare yourself for that freedom right now, I'd like you to finish this book with one more exercise.

MY FUTURE SELF

Read all through the exercise before you begin so that you are completely familiar with it.

1. Sit down somewhere quiet, where you won't be disturbed for ten minutes.
2. Close your eyes and paint a picture in your mind of yourself a few pounds lighter and just a little more relaxed and happy. Take all the time you need to do this, and let your unconscious mind help you.
3. When you are ready, step into your future, slimmer self – see from your future eyes, hear with your future ears and feel with your future body. Feel how your clothes are looser now. Relish this experience until you can feel it in every cell of your body, and notice exactly how it feels.
4. From this place, imagine another future where you are a few pounds lighter still. More happy, more confident and more relaxed, now wearing new, smaller clothes. Paint a really vivid picture of your future slimmer self.
5. Now step into this future, slimmer self. Notice how comfortable you feel, how relaxed you are and how much energy you have.

6. From this self, imagine yet another future self, now even lighter and slimmer and with the light of emotional wisdom shining in your eyes. Make the picture vivid and bright. Notice how you are standing and smiling. Notice how the future you is happy, energetic, slim and smiling.

7. When you are ready, step into this future self and enjoy every aspect of your wonderful self.

Working with your body

Now that you are working with your body and your emotions, you have the opportunity to be grateful for the amazing system that makes up the human being. You can appreciate and love this magnificent vehicle for your consciousness. The struggles and pain of the past are all changed, one bit at a time, into wisdom and insight that help you fully enjoy the present.

As you work through this system you will learn a great deal about yourself. You will also have a wonderful time and be amazed at how feelings that were once frightening are transformed by this process. At times it might seem like magic, but actually it is better than magic – it is your own achievement. You will deserve the success you achieve.

CHAPTER EIGHT

•

Success Tracker

SUCCESS TRACKER

If I were to give one piece of advice out of all I've learned and experienced in the field of personal change, I would say:

You get more of what you focus on.

I meet too many people who only tell me about their problems. When they start to tell me about their achievements – however small – I know they are on the road to success.

Use this journal to track your progress during the next four weeks.

Remember to follow the Golden Rules, use the Havening technique and, whenever you find emotions challenging, use the Five Questions. As you do that, you will naturally progress each day. The notes in this journal keep track of your progress. Write every day, and in the weeks and months ahead you will look back and be delighted to have a detailed record of your progress.

DAY 1

TODAY'S SUCCESS CHECKLIST

		TICK	COMMENT
1	I ate when I was hungry	☐	_____
2	I ate what I *really* wanted	☐	_____
3	I ate consciously	☐	_____
4	I stopped when full	☐	_____
5	I listened to the Hypnotic Trance CD	☐	_____
6	I used the 'Listen While You Eat' CD	☐	_____
7	I used the Havening DVD	☐	_____

TODAY I NOTICED THAT I FELT...

_____

_____

_____

TODAY I ALSO USED THE FOLLOWING TECHNIQUES
(tick those that apply)

Instant Calm	☐	Five Questions	☐
Stopping Self-sabotage	☐	Escape the Vortex	☐
Emotional Balancing	☐	My Future Self	☐

DAY 2

MY POSITIVE GOAL IS...

_____

_____

TODAY'S SUCCESS CHECKLIST

	TICK	COMMENT
1 I ate when I was hungry	☐	_____
2 I ate what I _really_ wanted	☐	_____
3 I ate consciously	☐	_____
4 I stopped when full	☐	_____
5 I listened to the Hypnotic Trance CD	☐	_____
6 I used the 'Listen While You Eat' CD	☐	_____
7 I used the Havening DVD	☐	_____

TODAY I NOTICED THAT I FELT...

_____

_____

_____

TODAY I ALSO USED THE FOLLOWING TECHNIQUES

(tick those that apply)

Instant Calm	☐	Five Questions	☐
Stopping Self-sabotage	☐	Escape the Vortex	☐
Emotional Balancing	☐	My Future Self	☐

DAY 3

MY POSITIVE GOAL IS…

_____

_____

TODAY'S SUCCESS CHECKLIST

		TICK	COMMENT
1	I ate when I was hungry	☐	_____
2	I ate what I _really_ wanted	☐	_____
3	I ate consciously	☐	_____
4	I stopped when full	☐	_____
5	I listened to the Hypnotic Trance CD	☐	_____
6	I used the 'Listen While You Eat' CD	☐	_____
7	I used the Havening DVD	☐	_____

TODAY I NOTICED THAT I FELT…

_____

_____

_____

TODAY I ALSO USED THE FOLLOWING TECHNIQUES
(tick those that apply)

Instant Calm   ☐   Five Questions   ☐

Stopping Self-sabotage   ☐   Escape the Vortex   ☐

Emotional Balancing   ☐   My Future Self   ☐

DAY 4

MY POSITIVE GOAL IS…

_____

_____

TODAY'S SUCCESS CHECKLIST

	TICK	COMMENT
1 I ate when I was hungry	☐	_____
2 I ate what I _really_ wanted	☐	_____
3 I ate consciously	☐	_____
4 I stopped when full	☐	_____
5 I listened to the Hypnotic Trance CD	☐	_____
6 I used the 'Listen While You Eat' CD	☐	_____
7 I used the Havening DVD	☐	_____

TODAY I NOTICED THAT I FELT…

_____

_____

_____

TODAY I ALSO USED THE FOLLOWING TECHNIQUES

(tick those that apply)

Instant Calm	☐	Five Questions	☐
Stopping Self-sabotage	☐	Escape the Vortex	☐
Emotional Balancing	☐	My Future Self	☐

DAY 5

MY POSITIVE GOAL IS...

_____

_____

TODAY'S SUCCESS CHECKLIST

	TICK	COMMENT
1 I ate when I was hungry	☐	_____
2 I ate what I _really_ wanted	☐	_____
3 I ate consciously	☐	_____
4 I stopped when full	☐	_____
5 I listened to the Hypnotic Trance CD	☐	_____
6 I used the 'Listen While You Eat' CD	☐	_____
7 I used the Havening DVD	☐	_____

TODAY I NOTICED THAT I FELT...

_____

_____

_____

TODAY I ALSO USED THE FOLLOWING TECHNIQUES
(tick those that apply)

Instant Calm	☐	Five Questions	☐
Stopping Self-sabotage	☐	Escape the Vortex	☐
Emotional Balancing	☐	My Future Self	☐

DAY 6

MY POSITIVE GOAL IS...

_____

_____

TODAY'S SUCCESS CHECKLIST

		TICK	COMMENT
1	I ate when I was hungry	☐	_____
2	I ate what I *really* wanted	☐	_____
3	I ate consciously	☐	_____
4	I stopped when full	☐	_____
5	I listened to the Hypnotic Trance CD	☐	_____
6	I used the 'Listen While You Eat' CD	☐	_____

TODAY I NOTICED THAT I FELT...

_____

_____

_____

TODAY I ALSO USED THE FOLLOWING TECHNIQUES

(tick those that apply)

Instant Calm	☐	Five Questions	☐
Stopping Self-sabotage	☐	Escape the Vortex	☐
Emotional Balancing	☐	My Future Self	☐
Havening	☐		

DAY 7

MY POSITIVE GOAL IS...

_____

_____

TODAY'S SUCCESS CHECKLIST

		TICK	COMMENT
1	I ate when I was hungry	☐	_____
2	I ate what I _really_ wanted	☐	_____
3	I ate consciously	☐	_____
4	I stopped when full	☐	_____
5	I listened to the Hypnotic Trance CD	☐	_____
6	I used the 'Listen While You Eat' CD	☐	_____

TODAY I NOTICED THAT I FELT...

_____

_____

_____

TODAY I ALSO USED THE FOLLOWING TECHNIQUES
(tick those that apply)

Instant Calm	☐	Five Questions	☐
Stopping Self-sabotage	☐	Escape the Vortex	☐
Emotional Balancing	☐	My Future Self	☐
Havening	☐		

DAY 8

MY POSITIVE GOAL IS...

_____

_____

TODAY'S SUCCESS CHECKLIST

		TICK	COMMENT
1	I ate when I was hungry	☐	_____
2	I ate what I *really* wanted	☐	_____
3	I ate consciously	☐	_____
4	I stopped when full	☐	_____

TODAY I NOTICED THAT I FELT...

_____

_____

_____

TODAY I ALSO USED THE FOLLOWING TECHNIQUES

(tick those that apply)

Instant Calm	☐	Five Questions	☐
Stopping Self-sabotage	☐	Escape the Vortex	☐
Emotional Balancing	☐	My Future Self	☐
'Listen While You Eat'	☐	Hypnotic Trance	☐
Havening	☐		

DAY 9

MY POSITIVE GOAL IS...

_____

_____

TODAY'S SUCCESS CHECKLIST

		TICK	COMMENT
1	I ate when I was hungry	☐	_____
2	I ate what I _really_ wanted	☐	_____
3	I ate consciously	☐	_____
4	I stopped when full	☐	_____

TODAY I NOTICED THAT I FELT...

_____

_____

_____

TODAY I ALSO USED THE FOLLOWING TECHNIQUES
(tick those that apply)

Instant Calm	☐	Five Questions	☐
Stopping Self-sabotage	☐	Escape the Vortex	☐
Emotional Balancing	☐	My Future Self	☐
'Listen While You Eat'	☐	Hypnotic Trance	☐
Havening	☐		

DAY 10

MY POSITIVE GOAL IS...

_____

_____

TODAY'S SUCCESS CHECKLIST

	TICK	COMMENT
1 I ate when I was hungry	☐	_____
2 I ate what I *really* wanted	☐	_____
3 I ate consciously	☐	_____
4 I stopped when full	☐	_____

TODAY I NOTICED THAT I FELT...

_____

_____

_____

TODAY I ALSO USED THE FOLLOWING TECHNIQUES

(tick those that apply)

Instant Calm	☐	Five Questions	☐
Stopping Self-sabotage	☐	Escape the Vortex	☐
Emotional Balancing	☐	My Future Self	☐
'Listen While You Eat'	☐	Hypnotic Trance	☐
Havening	☐		

DAY 11

MY POSITIVE GOAL IS...

_____

_____

TODAY'S SUCCESS CHECKLIST

	TICK	COMMENT
1 I ate when I was hungry	☐	_____
2 I ate what I _really_ wanted	☐	_____
3 I ate consciously	☐	_____
4 I stopped when full	☐	_____

TODAY I NOTICED THAT I FELT...

_____

_____

_____

TODAY I ALSO USED THE FOLLOWING TECHNIQUES
(tick those that apply)

Instant Calm	☐	Five Questions	☐
Stopping Self-sabotage	☐	Escape the Vortex	☐
Emotional Balancing	☐	My Future Self	☐
'Listen While You Eat'	☐	Hypnotic Trance	☐
Havening	☐		

DAY 12

MY POSITIVE GOAL IS...

_____

_____

TODAY'S SUCCESS CHECKLIST

	TICK	COMMENT
1 I ate when I was hungry	☐	_____
2 I ate what I *really* wanted	☐	_____
3 I ate consciously	☐	_____
4 I stopped when full	☐	_____

TODAY I NOTICED THAT I FELT...

_____

_____

_____

TODAY I ALSO USED THE FOLLOWING TECHNIQUES

(tick those that apply)

Instant Calm	☐	Five Questions	☐
Stopping Self-sabotage	☐	Escape the Vortex	☐
Emotional Balancing	☐	My Future Self	☐
'Listen While You Eat'	☐	Hypnotic Trance	☐
Havening	☐		

DAY 13

MY POSITIVE GOAL IS...

_____

_____

TODAY'S SUCCESS CHECKLIST

		TICK	COMMENT
1	I ate when I was hungry	☐	_____
2	I ate what I _really_ wanted	☐	_____
3	I ate consciously	☐	_____
4	I stopped when full	☐	_____

TODAY I NOTICED THAT I FELT...

_____

_____

_____

TODAY I ALSO USED THE FOLLOWING TECHNIQUES

(tick those that apply)

Instant Calm	☐	Five Questions	☐
Stopping Self-sabotage	☐	Escape the Vortex	☐
Emotional Balancing	☐	My Future Self	☐
'Listen While You Eat'	☐	Hypnotic Trance	☐
Havening	☐		

DAY 14

MY POSITIVE GOAL IS...

_____

_____

TODAY'S SUCCESS CHECKLIST

	TICK	COMMENT
1 I ate when I was hungry	☐	_____
2 I ate what I *really* wanted	☐	_____
3 I ate consciously	☐	_____
4 I stopped when full	☐	_____

TODAY I NOTICED THAT I FELT...

_____

_____

_____

TODAY I ALSO USED THE FOLLOWING TECHNIQUES
(tick those that apply)

Instant Calm	☐	Five Questions	☐
Stopping Self-sabotage	☐	Escape the Vortex	☐
Emotional Balancing	☐	My Future Self	☐
'Listen While You Eat'	☐	Hypnotic Trance	☐
Havening	☐		

DAY 15

MY POSITIVE GOAL IS...

_____

_____

TODAY'S SUCCESS CHECKLIST

	TICK	COMMENT
1 I ate when I was hungry	☐	_____
2 I ate what I _really_ wanted	☐	_____
3 I ate consciously	☐	_____
4 I stopped when full	☐	_____

TODAY I NOTICED THAT I FELT...

_____

_____

_____

TODAY I ALSO USED THE FOLLOWING TECHNIQUES
(tick those that apply)

Instant Calm	☐	Five Questions	☐
Stopping Self-sabotage	☐	Escape the Vortex	☐
Emotional Balancing	☐	My Future Self	☐
'Listen While You Eat'	☐	Hypnotic Trance	☐
Havening	☐		

DAY 16

MY POSITIVE GOAL IS...

_____

_____

TODAY'S SUCCESS CHECKLIST

	TICK	COMMENT
1 I ate when I was hungry	☐	_____
2 I ate what _really_ wanted	☐	_____
3 I ate consciously	☐	_____
4 I stopped when full	☐	_____

TODAY I NOTICED THAT I FELT...

_____

_____

_____

TODAY I ALSO USED THE FOLLOWING TECHNIQUES

(tick those that apply)

Instant Calm	☐	Five Questions	☐
Stopping Self-sabotage	☐	Escape the Vortex	☐
Emotional Balancing	☐	My Future Self	☐
'Listen While You Eat'	☐	Hypnotic Trance	☐
Havening	☐		

DAY 17

MY POSITIVE GOAL IS...

_____

_____

TODAY'S SUCCESS CHECKLIST

		TICK	COMMENT
1	I ate when I was hungry	☐	_____
2	I ate what I _really_ wanted	☐	_____
3	I ate consciously	☐	_____
4	I stopped when full	☐	_____

TODAY I NOTICED THAT I FELT...

_____

_____

_____

TODAY I ALSO USED THE FOLLOWING TECHNIQUES
(tick those that apply)

Instant Calm	☐	Five Questions	☐
Stopping Self-sabotage	☐	Escape the Vortex	☐
Emotional Balancing	☐	My Future Self	☐
'Listen While You Eat'	☐	Hypnotic Trance	☐
Havening	☐		

DAY 18

MY POSITIVE GOAL IS...

_____

_____

TODAY'S SUCCESS CHECKLIST

		TICK	COMMENT
1	I ate when I was hungry	☐	_____
2	I ate what I _really_ wanted	☐	_____
3	I ate consciously	☐	_____
4	I stopped when full	☐	_____

TODAY I NOTICED THAT I FELT...

_____

_____

_____

TODAY I ALSO USED THE FOLLOWING TECHNIQUES

(tick those that apply)

Instant Calm	☐	Five Questions	☐
Stopping Self-sabotage	☐	Escape the Vortex	☐
Emotional Balancing	☐	My Future Self	☐
'Listen While You Eat'	☐	Hypnotic Trance	☐
Havening	☐		

DAY 19

MY POSITIVE GOAL IS...

_____

_____

TODAY'S SUCCESS CHECKLIST

		TICK	COMMENT
1	I ate when I was hungry	☐	_____
2	I ate what I _really_ wanted	☐	_____
3	I ate consciously	☐	_____
4	I stopped when full	☐	_____

TODAY I NOTICED THAT I FELT...

_____

_____

_____

TODAY I ALSO USED THE FOLLOWING TECHNIQUES

(tick those that apply)

Instant Calm	☐	Five Questions	☐
Stopping Self-sabotage	☐	Escape the Vortex	☐
Emotional Balancing	☐	My Future Self	☐
'Listen While You Eat'	☐	Hypnotic Trance	☐
Havening	☐		

DAY 20

MY POSITIVE GOAL IS...

_____

_____

TODAY'S SUCCESS CHECKLIST

		TICK	COMMENT
1	I ate when I was hungry	☐	_____
2	I ate what I *really* wanted	☐	_____
3	I ate consciously	☐	_____
4	I stopped when full	☐	_____

TODAY I NOTICED THAT I FELT...

_____

_____

_____

TODAY I ALSO USED THE FOLLOWING TECHNIQUES
(tick those that apply)

Instant Calm	☐	Five Questions	☐
Stopping Self-sabotage	☐	Escape the Vortex	☐
Emotional Balancing	☐	My Future Self	☐
'Listen While You Eat'	☐	Hypnotic Trance	☐
Havening	☐		

DAY 21

MY POSITIVE GOAL IS...

_____

_____

TODAY'S SUCCESS CHECKLIST

		TICK	COMMENT
1	I ate when I was hungry	☐	_____
2	I ate what I _really_ wanted	☐	_____
3	I ate consciously	☐	_____
4	I stopped when full	☐	_____

TODAY I NOTICED THAT I FELT...

_____

_____

_____

TODAY I ALSO USED THE FOLLOWING TECHNIQUES
(tick those that apply)

Instant Calm	☐	Five Questions	☐
Stopping Self-sabotage	☐	Escape the Vortex	☐
Emotional Balancing	☐	My Future Self	☐
'Listen While You Eat'	☐	Hypnotic Trance	☐
Havening	☐		

DAY 22

MY POSITIVE GOAL IS...

_____

_____

TODAY'S SUCCESS CHECKLIST

		TICK	COMMENT
1	I ate when I was hungry	☐	_____
2	I ate what I _really_ wanted	☐	_____
3	I ate consciously	☐	_____
4	I stopped when full	☐	_____

TODAY I NOTICED THAT I FELT...

_____

_____

_____

TODAY I ALSO USED THE FOLLOWING TECHNIQUES

(tick those that apply)

Instant Calm	☐	Five Questions	☐
Stopping Self-sabotage	☐	Escape the Vortex	☐
Emotional Balancing	☐	My Future Self	☐
'Listen While You Eat'	☐	Hypnotic Trance	☐
Havening	☐		

DAY 23

MY POSITIVE GOAL IS...

_____

_____

TODAY'S SUCCESS CHECKLIST

		TICK	COMMENT
1	I ate when I was hungry	☐	_____
2	I ate what I _really_ wanted	☐	_____
3	I ate consciously	☐	_____
4	I stopped when full	☐	_____

TODAY I NOTICED THAT I FELT...

_____

_____

_____

TODAY I ALSO USED THE FOLLOWING TECHNIQUES
(tick those that apply)

Instant Calm	☐	Five Questions	☐
Stopping Self-sabotage	☐	Escape the Vortex	☐
Emotional Balancing	☐	My Future Self	☐
'Listen While You Eat'	☐	Hypnotic Trance	☐
Havening	☐		

DAY 24

MY POSITIVE GOAL IS...

_____

_____

TODAY'S SUCCESS CHECKLIST

	TICK	COMMENT
1 I ate when I was hungry	☐	_____
2 I ate what I *really* wanted	☐	_____
3 I ate consciously	☐	_____
4 I stopped when full	☐	_____

TODAY I NOTICED THAT I FELT...

_____

_____

_____

TODAY I ALSO USED THE FOLLOWING TECHNIQUES

(tick those that apply)

Instant Calm	☐	Five Questions	☐
Stopping Self-sabotage	☐	Escape the Vortex	☐
Emotional Balancing	☐	My Future Self	☐
'Listen While You Eat'	☐	Hypnotic Trance	☐
Havening	☐		

DAY 25

MY POSITIVE GOAL IS…

_____

_____

TODAY'S SUCCESS CHECKLIST

		TICK	COMMENT
1	I ate when I was hungry	☐	_____
2	I ate what I *really* wanted	☐	_____
3	I ate consciously	☐	_____
4	I stopped when full	☐	_____

TODAY I NOTICED THAT I FELT…

_____

_____

_____

TODAY I ALSO USED THE FOLLOWING TECHNIQUES
(tick those that apply)

Instant Calm	☐	Five Questions	☐
Stopping Self-sabotage	☐	Escape the Vortex	☐
Emotional Balancing	☐	My Future Self	☐
'Listen While You Eat'	☐	Hypnotic Trance	☐
Havening	☐		

DAY 26

MY POSITIVE GOAL IS...

_____

_____

TODAY'S SUCCESS CHECKLIST

		TICK	COMMENT
1	I ate when I was hungry	☐	_____
2	I ate what I *really* wanted	☐	_____
3	I ate consciously	☐	_____
4	I stopped when full	☐	_____

TODAY I NOTICED THAT I FELT...

_____

_____

_____

TODAY I ALSO USED THE FOLLOWING TECHNIQUES

(tick those that apply)

Instant Calm	☐	Five Questions	☐
Stopping Self-sabotage	☐	Escape the Vortex	☐
Emotional Balancing	☐	My Future Self	☐
'Listen While You Eat'	☐	Hypnotic Trance	☐
Havening	☐		

DAY 27

MY POSITIVE GOAL IS...

_____

_____

TODAY'S SUCCESS CHECKLIST

		TICK	COMMENT
1	I ate when I was hungry	☐	_____
2	I ate what I _really_ wanted	☐	_____
3	I ate consciously	☐	_____
4	I stopped when full	☐	_____

TODAY I NOTICED THAT I FELT...

_____

_____

_____

TODAY I ALSO USED THE FOLLOWING TECHNIQUES

(tick those that apply)

Instant Calm	☐	Five Questions	☐
Stopping Self-sabotage	☐	Escape the Vortex	☐
Emotional Balancing	☐	My Future Self	☐
'Listen While You Eat'	☐	Hypnotic Trance	☐
Havening	☐		

DAY 28

MY POSITIVE GOAL IS...

_____

_____

TODAY'S SUCCESS CHECKLIST

	TICK	COMMENT
1 I ate when I was hungry	☐	_____
2 I ate what I _really_ wanted	☐	_____
3 I ate consciously	☐	_____
4 I stopped when full	☐	_____

TODAY I NOTICED THAT I FELT...

_____

_____

_____

TODAY I ALSO USED THE FOLLOWING TECHNIQUES
(tick those that apply)

Instant Calm	☐	Five Questions	☐
Stopping Self-sabotage	☐	Escape the Vortex	☐
Emotional Balancing	☐	My Future Self	☐
'Listen While You Eat'	☐	Hypnotic Trance	☐
Havening	☐		

When you have reached the end of the month, if you would like to carry on, buy yourself a small notebook and write something each day. You will find that your eating changes radically within the first four weeks, but carry on making notes until you feel you are fully and completely established in eating according to the Four Golden Rules.

Carry on writing about what you feel for as long as you wish, because the process of unfolding your emotions can go on for a long time. It becomes a wonderful journey of self-discovery, which is worth documenting.

A PERSONAL MESSAGE FROM PAUL

I wish you all the very best on your journey to a richer, more fulfilling version of your life. I have included many ideas and exercises in this book because I want to be one hundred per cent certain that you have all you need to overcome emotional eating, lose weight and have real emotional freedom and control.

At the core of this system are five things you need to do:

1. **Use the Hypnotic Trance on the CD.**
2. **Use the Havening DVD.**
3. **Use the Five Questions to process your emotions (see page 113).**
4. **Use the 'Listen While You Eat' track on the CD.**
5. **Follow the Four Golden Rules (see pages 67–83).**

You are now well on the way to a fundamental change in your thinking and behaviour around food, and to a richer, more rewarding emotional life. I congratulate you!

Until we meet,

Paul McKenna

ACKNOWLEDGEMENTS

Dr Richard Bandler, Deborah Tom, Professor Neil Greenberg, Genpo Roshi, Mari Roberts, Gillian Blease, Julia Lloyd, Doug Young, Mike Osborne, Alex Bushe, Kate Davey, Alex Tuppen and Steve Shaw.

Special thanks to:

Dr Ronald Ruden, whose wisdom, intellect and tireless dedication to helping making the lives of other people better is a constant source of inspiration to me.

Dr Hugh Willbourn, whose astounding work ethic and attention to detail makes him a privilege to work with.

Finally, and very importantly, thank you to all the people who have participated in the numerous Havening research studies over the last few years, courageously allowing me to join them, at times in the depths of emotional despair, and giving me the honour of helping them return from the darkest places, making it possible for others to do so, too – I have the utmost respect for you.